GOD STILL SPEAKS

THROUGH

DREAMS

OTHER BOOKS AND PRODUCTS BY GREG CYNAUMON

The Barnes and Noble Bible Trivia Quiz Book
Left Behind—The Board Game Adventure
Empowering Single Parents
How to Avoid Alienating Your Kids in 10 Easy Steps

Dr. Cynaumon can be reached via www.dreamfocus.org

GOD STILL SPEAKS THROUGH
DREAMS

ARE YOU MISSING HIS MESSAGES?

DR. GREG CYNAUMON

THOMAS NELSON PUBLISHERS®
Nashville

A Division of Thomas Nelson, Inc.
www.ThomasNelson.com

Published in Nashville, Tennessee, by Thomas Nelson, Inc.

Published in association with the literary agency of Alive Communications, 7680 Goddard Street, Suite 200, Colorado Springs, CO 80920.

Scripture quotations are taken from the HOLY BIBLE: NEW INTERNATIONAL VERSION®. Copyright © 1973, 1978, 1984 by International Bible Society. Used by permission of Zondervan Publishing House. All rights reserved.

ISBN 13: 978-0-7852-9683-6

Printed in the United States of America

02 03 04 05 06 BVG 5 4 3 2 1

To Jan

CONTENTS

ACKNOWLEDGMENTS

Sometimes the joy of writing is compromised through the sacrifice of time with one's family and friends. Only through the grace of Jesus and loved ones does the writing experience truly become joyful. That is why I dedicate this book to my wife, Jan—who is as supportive as she is inwardly and outwardly beautiful.

To my daughter (excuse me, Senior Class President), Tracy, and my son, Matt (the three-sport letterman—there, bragging is over), thanks for enriching my life daily by joining us at the "bagel place" before school to kid around over breakfast. You make parenting fun!

To my remarkable parents, Myrna and Ed, and my brother Dana and his wife, Pam—let me simply say thanks for being there!

To all those who were instrumental in bringing this book to fruition: Chip MacGregor, my agent and confidant at Alive Communications—thanks for your diligence. To the Thomas Nelson team captained by Brian Hampton and Kyle Olund, thanks for your courage and for sharing the dream (pun intended). And to Marie Prys and Mark Calkins, and Dr. Mike Kogutek . . . thank you for your encouragement and keen editing eyes.

INTRODUCTION

Over the span of one month, the young police officer was troubled by a recurring nightmare, causing him to awaken in a panic at least two nights a week. In his nightmare the officer was in foot pursuit of various criminals. Some nights they were murderers or rapists. Other nights they were burglars or robbers. It never seemed to matter what their particular criminal behavior was because the dreams always ended in the particularly bloody and painful gunshot death of the officer.

As the officer would later learn, it was not a completely unique dream to law enforcement officers. Cops are renowned for vivid and lucid nightmares revolving around their violent professions, but this one had some unusual twists and turns.

In his recurring nightmare he chased the suspect down a long, dark alley, gaining ground with each stride. In dream after dream the suspect was just far enough ahead so that when he rounded the corner of a building, he disappeared momentarily from view. The final dream sequence always started with the policeman following the suspect around the corner of the building only to find the suspect stopped and aiming a weapon at the officer.

As a sense of panic set in, the young officer drew his revolver from its holster. Both officer and suspect squared off, facing each other with barely ten feet separating them. Suddenly both fired their weapons at precisely the same second. And that was where the nightmare took an even more curious turn.

In his dream the young officer observed an odd fact. He was not wearing his department's standard blue uniform worn by everyone. Instead, he was wearing a tan shirt and green pants, the uniform uniquely worn by the county's sheriff deputies. His dream continued as he fired his chrome 9 mm

Smith and Wesson at such close range that he knew the bullet would find its mark. He felt the weapon recoil in his hand, but something was strangely different. The high-powered 9 mm didn't feel at all like it did when he practiced on the police target range. It felt light, almost hollow. As the 9 mm bullet fired, it didn't return its usual ear-piercing report. It sounded more like a Fourth of July firecracker.

The officer stood transfixed as the suspect looked down the sight of his handgun, which was pointed at the officer's face. With the steely calmness of a seasoned killer, the suspect squeezed the trigger and fired a round. Squared off and separated by ten feet, both suspect and officer had fired their weapons, but what was about to happen to the patrolman separated his nightmare from most police-related dreams.

A small puff of white smoke emerged from the barrel of the officer's handgun while a large plume of black smoke exited the suspect's handgun along with the deadly bullet. The officer's bullet began to slow as it left the barrel and assumed almost a surreal, slow motion as it moved toward the suspect. In stark contrast, the suspect's bullet was traveling at an extreme velocity as it sped toward the young officer. The officer was playing a waiting game as he frantically anticipated which bullet would find its target first. Seconds dragged out like minutes, and the officer's anxiety mounted. The bullet from his weapon inched toward the suspect and slowed to such an extent that it began to arc downward. Finally devoid of velocity, the officer's bullet fell passively at the suspect's feet. Conversely the suspect's bullet reached a blinding speed and found its target—the officer's mouth. The officer stood for a moment, staring in amazement at what had just transpired before collapsing to die an agonizing death at the feet of the laughing suspect.

Desperate to try to understand the meaning of his dream, the young officer cautiously revealed it to a select few fellow officers whom he hoped might help him to unlock its hidden meaning. In typical cop "gallows" humor, his comrades laughed and made light of his dream. The responses he received ranged from laughter to suggestions he check himself into the psycho ward. Only one officer, a friend and fellow academy graduate who worked for the Sheriff's Department, seemed to understand and sympathize with how disturbing the dream was. In place of the usual uncomfortable laughter, which often accompanied sensitive discussions around police officers, his friend nodded and admitted to having a similar dream once, but he had passed it off.

Reluctantly heeding the advice of his friend, the officer made an appointment to see the department's psychologist. The psychologist listened intently and did his best to help, but he had little understanding of the dream's meaning—much less how he could provide the young officer with any relief. Largely untrained in dream awareness or interpretation, the doctor had only a hunch that the dream probably had something to do with the stress that police officers feel in a high-risk profession. His parting advice was to try to put it out of mind and understand that it was merely a dream. The psychologist nevertheless provided the troubled officer with a business card of a colleague who specialized in dream analysis—just in case he wanted to explore the dream further.

Several nights passed without the horrible recurring nightmare, and the officer thought his brief visit to the department psychologist had done the trick. But after a particularly stressful shift, the nightmare returned to torment him once again. The next day, the officer called to schedule an appointment with the doctor whom the department psychologist had recommended.

The doctor looked precisely the way the young officer had envisioned he would. He was a man in his mid- to late sixties, bald, except for a few wispy strands of white hair, and dressed in a gray flannel suit. His comfortable office exuded inviting warmth with its wood paneling and soft leather furniture. The officer walked in, took a seat on the couch, and proceeded to tell the psychologist his recurring nightmare.

Listening intently while making a few notes, the psychologist said nothing until the young officer had finished recounting his chilling nightmare. The psychologist then asked, "What is your concern about the weapon you carry on duty?"

Surprised momentarily, the officer replied, "The department changed its policy about six months ago. Before, we all carried .357 magnum revolvers, but the brass decided to issue 9 mm semiautomatics for some reason. The only exception was if you wanted to buy your own gun. Then they'll let you carry a .45."

"I know nothing about handguns, but what did you think about giving up your .357 magnum for the 9 mm gun the department issued?" inquired the psychologist.

"I guess I wasn't too happy about it," replied the officer.

"Why?" he fired back.

"Because in the police academy, we had seen these tests done. They took human-size gelatin molds and fired rounds into them to see what effect different bullets would have on a human-size mass," explained the officer.

"And what was the outcome?" asked the psychologist like a lion stalking its prey.

"They found that the best ammunition for law enforcement was .45 caliber or .357 magnum because each had more knockdown power than 9 mm or .38 caliber bullets," the officer replied.

"Then why did your department switch to 9 mm if they knew it wasn't as effective as .357 or .45 caliber?" he inquired of the officer.

"Well, I think it was because 9 mm's are magazine fed, and tests showed that officers are often shot while trying to reload their revolvers, which hold only six rounds," responded the officer.

"So, did you tell anyone you were not in favor of switching to the 9 mm?" the doctor persisted.

"Well . . . no," stated the officer. "It's just not my place—being a rookie and all. Questioning department policies would be like committing career suicide."

Easing back in his leather recliner, the psychologist prepared to make sense of the dream that had haunted the young officer. Slowly and precisely the psychologist began to speak: "Please allow me to make some sense of it for you. The symbol of your bullet in your dream is no mystery at all. This represents your well-grounded anxiety that you are carrying a weapon that is less than adequate. One that, in fact, places you in harm's way, no?"

Refining his interpretation, the psychologist continued, "The fact that each nightmare features a suspect who squares off with you in what one might term a 'duel to the death' tells me that you believe the bad guys have superior weapons and therefore have less to fear from you than you from them."

Closing his eyes as if to increase his focus to the hidden essence and meaning of the recurring nightmares, the veteran doctor concluded his analysis: "The reason that each nightmare concludes with your being shot in the mouth is truly significant. This is a dream symbol that signifies your sense of forced silence and powerlessness over being made to change to a substandard weapon. That much is apparent."

With a strange expression and furrowed brow the doctor asked, "There is one perplexing aspect of the dream that does not make sense to me. Perhaps you can elaborate. You say you are not wearing your own uniform but are instead dressed in the uniform of a deputy sheriff, correct?"

"That's right," he replied, "but I've never worn that kind of uniform."

"The fact that you've never worn that uniform catches my attention. Do you have any friends who wear that uniform currently, or were you ever involved in a shooting alongside deputies who wore that uniform?" the doctor inquired.

Flashing back to the conversation he had with his friend about his dream, the officer told the doctor about his academy classmate who worked for the Sheriff's Department. He also told the doctor that his friend had revealed once experiencing a similar dream.

Drawing a breath as if preparing for a difficult revelation, the psychologist began slowly. "I think your dream presents two distinct images that I'd like you to consider carefully. The first is that your dream is your subconscious mind's way of forcing you to deal with your anxiety over an inferior weapon. If this is the case, then your path is simple. You voice your feelings to your superiors about the weapon, or you purchase a weapon more of your own choosing. If that is the origin of your recurring nightmares, then we have solved the riddle, and they should go away. Simple, no?" he asked, although it wasn't really a question.

"I can do that," the officer said resolutely, sensing there was a bigger issue coming.

"I also want you to consider a different possibility about your dream," the doctor said while leaning forward to the edge of his chair. "Are you a religious man?" he inquired.

"Yes, as a matter of fact, I am," the officer replied.

Cocking his head slightly to the side, the doctor asked, "Have you prayed about your dream or asked for God to reveal its meaning to you?"

"Absolutely," the officer answered. "Every time I have one of those nightmares, I pray about it and then try to go back to sleep."

"In that case I want you to consider warning your deputy sheriff friend that there is at least a possibility that you are a messenger who has been given a dream that was meant as a warning for him."

With a look of bewilderment, the officer voiced his thoughts: "Are you telling me that you think I'm not myself in my dream, that I'm actually my buddy, and that this is all about warning him of something that's about to happen?"

"I'm not here to tell you what to do," replied the doctor. "I'm only here to interpret and suggest to the best of my ability. If you are a spiritual man, then surely you have read multiple scriptures where God delivered dreams and visions to plain and ordinary men. I myself have had patients who've had dream premonitions that have come true. I'm not telling you that your dream is God's way of warning your friend, but how would you feel if you said nothing and a tragedy occurred?"

‖   ‖   ‖

After submitting the matter to God in prayer, the patrolman decided to follow both of the doctor's suggestions. He received permission from the department to purchase a .45 caliber handgun and immediately felt a sense that he had done the right thing. But then he had to get to the awkward business of talking to his friend.

The next afternoon, he called his deputy friend, and the two of them met for a cup of coffee. Almost apologetically the officer reminded his friend of the dream he had shared with him before and added that he had since seen a doctor for advice. Although the friend didn't place much stock in premonitions, the deputy listened intently and thanked the young officer for caring. He did at least promise to think it over.

Several days passed without the recurring dream haunting the officer. *I guess the old guy was right, and switching weapons did the trick,* he thought. Then he got a phone call from his friend.

With a shaky tone, the deputy told the young officer of an incident the night before. He said he and two other officers were chasing a robbery suspect through an industrial complex when a strange sensation came over him, causing him to flash back to the dream conversation they'd had.

"We split up, and I followed the suspect while the other deputies cut through a walkway. I saw the suspect turn the corner of a building about fifty yards in front of me, but just then I actually had a flash, a mental image or something, of me lying dead on the sidewalk," he stammered. "So I stopped running and started creeping toward the corner of the building. I wasn't ten feet away when I heard the other deputies order the suspect to drop his weapon. When we got back to the station, the arresting deputy told me the suspect was just waiting for me to round that corner, and he would've had me."

"So are you okay?" interrupted the young officer.

"Yeah, I'm fine," the deputy replied. "But if I ever pop into another one of your dreams, promise me—day or night—you'll call me."

Whether it was changing weapons or warning the deputy that did the trick, the old doctor was right. The young officer never had that nightmare again.

THREE KINDS OF READERS

By now you may have surmised that I was that young officer. I understand that as you read my story and the other stories here, you'll likely fall into one of three camps. The first is comprised of spiritually minded people who have no difficulty in believing that God is sovereign and can do anything He chooses to do. They believe that He used dreams to communicate in the Bible, making it possible (if not probable) that He also uses dreams today. If this sounds like what you think, then the questions you should seek answers to are: How often does this indeed happen, and how can I tell if a dream is divine? More on those points later.

Or perhaps you belong to the second camp, a group that I refer to as *seekers*. Seekers are also spiritually minded, but they have a tougher time accepting spiritual phenomena such as angel appearances, miracles, demon possession, and the like. I definitely fall into this category, where the mind-set is *I'm open to understanding it, but I need evidence*. Seekers understand that dreams are the subconscious mind's way of dealing with leftover thoughts and emotions, but they're also open to the possibility that dreams could be divinely inspired.

A third group is drawn to the subject of dreams out of pure curiosity. These people are not particularly spiritually or psychologically minded. They tend to read about dreams because they find the topic interesting—even if they are nothing more than random movie clips played during sleep.

If you fall into one of these three camps, I humbly believe you will find the accompanying pages to be inspiring, informative, or—at the least—entertaining.

One final note: you should know that I believe my police dream *was* divinely inspired. That experience ignited my fascination with dreams and propelled me along my spiritual and scientific investigation into the subject. *I also firmly believe, and will make the case throughout the book, that we may very well be missing God's messages in our dreams.*

NEVER ACCEPT ADVICE FROM A LUNATIC

If you're like me, you want to know something about a person before you accept all that he is saying as truth, much less as biblical truth. What if I am a card-carrying lunatic who sits on hillsides baying at the full moon? Wouldn't you want to know that before you bought into my religious and scientific theories about dreams? I would.

To the best of my knowledge, I am not, nor have I ever been, a lunatic. My first and only wife of twenty-two years would tell you that although I may stare at the moon on occasion, I never bark. Since I am a straight-arrow ex-cop, you may surmise that I've never smoked pot, dropped acid, snorted cocaine, or shot heroin. The strongest drug I use is aspirin, and two of them give me a stomachache.

I should also assure you that I do not own a Ouija board, magic crystals, tarot cards, or tea leaves. I've never been to a psychic, numerologist, mystic, fortune-teller, exorcist, or spiritual medium. In fact, I'm not even too keen on chiropractors. Not because they are bad folks at all, but only because I avoid pain whenever possible. I don't read my horoscope, and I've never had an out-of-body experience or been accused of harboring demons.

You need to know that for the past eleven years, I have regularly attended and have been on the lay pastoral staff of a mainstream, evangelical, Bible-teaching church. For years I've taught adult Sunday school and been a featured lecturer in churches all around the country.

My spiritual beliefs revolve around Jesus Christ and my understanding that He was born of a miracle birth by the Virgin Mary, died on the cross for our sins, was resurrected, and then ascended to heaven. I also believe that He will return one day to fulfill the prophecies of the Bible.

So, should this information alone give you the confidence to accept what I'm saying as the gospel? Of course not. Test what I am teaching against the Bible. Talk with other religious and nonreligious people to get their position on this subject. Pray about dreams to try to get a sense of God's leading. Ultimately the decision is yours.

A LITTLE MORE BACKGROUND

While in my fifth (of a total of ten) year of law enforcement, I returned to college to study psychology. Throughout school, and in graduate school in particular, I found the study of dreams utterly fascinating. I took every opportunity to delve deeper into this mysterious topic, including studying under a prototypical Freudian dream analyst. In spite of gaining rich clinical knowledge from my secular and humanistic mentor, I found the experience to be limited only because it was so godless.

Never in classical secular dream analysis is there room for even a conversation about the idea that God might be communicating to people through their dreams. After all, how could God communicate through dreams when God does not exist? That would be like watching the TV when it's off.

Clearly if I wanted to examine dreams and dream symbols from an evangelical Christian perspective, the burden would be on me, and perhaps a few others, to integrate dream psychology with scripturally grounded theology.

Throughout my years of clinical practice, I have used dream analysis as a pivotal tool in helping my patients to gain a fuller understanding of what the unconscious mind was revealing. Between 5 and 10 percent of the dream cases I've studied appeared to be examples of divine intervention. By this, I mean that either God Himself spoke through the dream or He had His hand in it in some form. The most common among this category would be what people described as being visited by angels in their dreams. The trouble with divine dreams is that they come with no verifiable, scientific proof. It would be much simpler if God would just send His dreams with a letter of authenticity. Therefore, the scientist in me requires other forms of verification, which we will discuss in greater depth throughout the book.

Does God Still Speak Through Dreams?

Remember, a moment ago I told you that I consider myself a *seeker.* Let me give you an example of what I mean by that term. Even though I've never encountered an angel (as far as I know), I believe they exist because the Bible says so. The same holds true with miracles. The Bible tells us that both angels and miracles are from God, and we accept that, even though most of us (to our knowledge) have never witnessed either one.

For most people, dreams fall into a different category. The actual words *dream(s)* and *visions* appear 210 times in a standard New International Version Bible. The words *angel* and *angels* appear 215 times. And yet if you were to ask the average Christian whether angels or dreams seem more likely to come from God, the hands-down response would be angels. My point is not to diminish the role of angels and miracles in biblical times or even today. My point is that people flock to angel sightings and label various occurrences as miracles without a degree of skepticism. On the other hand, dreams and visions have been largely overlooked.

As a clinician, I have no doubts about the power of dreams and the benefits of understanding them. As a Christian, however, I must confess that I once viewed the subject of dreams with some degree of skepticism. After all, the New Age movement has adopted dreams as its own and seemingly frightened religiously minded people away. This is particularly sad in light of the number of times God spoke to people through dreams in the Bible and the promise He made that dreams and visions will play a particular role in the prediction of end-times events (Acts 2:17).

As Christians, we are commanded to judge all spiritual issues through the prism of 1 John 4:1–3:

> Dear friends, do not believe every spirit, but test the spirits to see whether they are from God, because many false prophets have gone out into the world. This is how you can recognize the Spirit of God: Every spirit that acknowledges that Jesus Christ has come in the flesh is from God, but every spirit that does not acknowledge Jesus is not from God. This is the spirit of the antichrist, which you have heard is coming and even now is already in the world.

This passage directs us to "test the spirits" to determine what is truly of God and what is not. I will not consider that a dream is divinely inspired unless it passes the test of scriptural scrutiny.

CHECK MY SOURCES

Over the years, I have challenged myself, and have been challenged by others, on the question of whether God speaks through dreams today. I believe He does, and I think the stories in this book will convince you as well. The only hesitation I have in taking such a definitive position is that I am concerned some might take it to the extreme and conclude that God speaks through *all* dreams. Having studied more than one thousand dreams, I found no evidence that God speaks through even a majority of dreams, let alone all of them.

The dreams selected for this book are some of the more vivid examples, the kind that led me to the conclusion that God does, in fact, speak through our dreams. This compilation comes from more than ten years of research and three main sources. The first source is my private practice. I have taken great care to conceal the identities of the individuals in order to preserve patient-doctor confidentiality. The second source is my daily radio show in southern California, for which I documented several hundred dreams. In many of these cases, I interviewed the caller "off air" to verify claims and to substantiate the credibility. Perhaps it is the old cop in me, coupled with the science-driven side of my brain, but I believe it is my obligation to present dreams only from sources I believe are credible. The third source of dream material is the countless lectures I have delivered on this topic. Often people approach me following a seminar to discuss a dream. Again, the dreams in this book came from people I looked upon as credible.

WHY ARE YOU READING THIS BOOK?

People pick up books on dreams for two reasons I want to highlight. The first is that they are scientifically and/or psychologically minded and enjoy exploring dry, unemotional psychological theses on dreams. If this describes you, you've definitely come to the wrong place. Although I absolutely consider myself a logical-thinking, left brain–leaning scientist, I did not set out to write another mundane dream study in hopes of it landing in some psychological journal to be read by two pointy-headed shrinks. Trust me when I say there are enough dream journals, books, manuals, encyclopedias, and articles to choke all of Freud's horses.

Still others may have been attracted to the word *God* in the title (note capital *G*, as in *the* God) and may be anticipating a New Age thesis on how we're all gods (note lowercase *g*) and are therefore able to direct our lives through our dreams. That is crystal-clutching balderdash! I disdain the fact that Christians have abandoned the domain of dreams to the New Age movement. If this is your bias, in all due respect, you have come to the wrong place. I'd love for you to read this book, but afterward I encourage you to visit an evangelical Christian church in your neighborhood. In doing that, more than anything else, you will gain a far better understanding of where I am coming from.

I must restate my unwavering bias to the fact that God is not only the Creator of heaven and earth, but He is also the original Author of dreams. Throughout this book, you will find my conclusion on the relationship between God and the dreamer to be consistent. Simply stated: God, since the beginning of time, has demonstrated a willingness to communicate with people through dreams. Some dreamers were great and powerful biblical figures fulfilling huge responsibilities in the shaping of history. Others were everyday people like you and me. They played minor roles in Scripture, other than their connection to the dream or the dreamer.

The bottom line is to keep an open mind about dreams and their meanings because only two possibilities are at work here. The first is that you orchestrate your own dreams. In this scenario, it's helpful to understand your dream in order to uncover and understand your subconscious thoughts and anxieties. I will submit to you that even if you are not completely comfortable with the premise that God can communicate through dreams today, perhaps an easier acceptance is that God created us with the ability to dream. Think about that for a moment. He created our minds in such a fashion to allow us to access information—hidden, repressed, or otherwise—while we sleep! Even if God is not on the other end of the dream, your ability to tap into your collective subconscious is possible because He deemed it so.

The second possibility, of course, is that God is speaking to you through your dreams. I assert that when that happens, you don't want to be asleep at the switch. If, in fact, God does choose to communicate to us through our dreams, I'm certain there is a perfect reason for it. Perhaps the distraction of our daily routine disconnects us from Him in such a manner that we don't hear Him.

An analogy might be the studies conducted with hospitalized patients who are in comas. Case after case concluded that many of them, even those with marginal brain wave activity due to cerebral trauma, can hear people around them speaking to them. If science has proven that the mind is capable of listening while unconscious, traumatized, or anesthetized, then why would it be difficult to believe our minds can hear God while we're asleep?

STARTING OFF WITH A DREAM PARABLE

A colleague tells the story about the most curious patient he has ever encountered. His patient showed up for his first appointment, handed the doctor a check for $150, told him about a problem he was having, and then leaned back and closed his eyes. My friend, believing his patient was merely resting his eyes, spoke and offered solutions for quite some time. In fact, the doctor shared his monologue right up to the time the man began snoring loudly.

Insulted at first, the doctor decided to let his patient sleep. After all, it was the patient's money, and if he wanted to waste his hour sleeping, well, that was his business. When the session was over, my colleague awakened the patient, who thanked the doctor and scheduled another appointment. The same scenario continued for the next two weeks until finally the doctor told his patient he could not, in good conscience, continue to take his money. He also asked the patient why he slept through the entire session each week. Reluctantly the patient told the doctor that although he had absolutely no interest in coming to counseling, his wife had insisted he attend or she would leave him. When the doctor suggested that, had he stayed awake, he might have solved some of his problems, the patient replied, "No offense, Doc, but I need sleep more than I need solutions."

In an abstract way, this is what happens to most spiritual people each night. We say our prayers before bed and ask God for His help and guidance in our lives. Then we drift off to sleep where we experience multiple dreams. The chances are good that at least one of our dreams revolved around the very concern we submitted to God earlier. The point is, if we don't remember or understand our dreams, we inadvertently act much like the slumbering patient. When that happens, we miss out in two significant ways. At the very least we lose the chance for the subconscious to offer some clear-thinking solutions to our daily dilemmas. But far more important, we cut ourselves off from God and the possibility that He has blessed us by providing the answer to the dilemma. Like the sleeping patient, we lose either way.

THE

DREAM

CHRONICLES

CASE NOTES:

The Drowning Dream

NAME: David
AGE: 42
OCCUPATION: Senior pastor
MARITAL STATUS: Married 15 years, with 3 children
(ages 13, 11, and 9)

In September of 1998, during my radio program, I received a call from a pastor by the name of David, who related a disturbing dream that he'd been struggling to understand for several weeks.

David's dream involved one of his children, which as many parents have experienced is the most disturbing type of dream imaginable. This pastor's dream, however, held a strange twist for my audience and me.

Pastor David described the evening leading up to his nightmare as uneventful. He and his wife had followed their usual routine that night, which consisted of watching the ten o'clock news and then going to sleep by 10:45 P.M. As his digital bedside clock clicked 11:23 P.M., the pastor was violently awakened from what he termed a "dead" sleep by the most gut-wrenching nightmare he had ever experienced.

"In my dream, my eleven-year-old son and I were up at our church retreat in the Sequoia Mountains. We had been there several times so I knew that was where my dream took place. I wish I could get this image out of my mind," he continued. "It's like it is indelibly etched into my brain—this mental image of my son's struggle," he trailed off.

"In my nightmare, I was standing on the edge of the water watching my

3

son and a neighbor boy paddling a canoe around the lake. For no reason at all, the neighbor boy stood up and started messing around as though he was going to tip the canoe. The problem is, my son is a fine swimmer in real life, but I know for a fact that the neighbor boy can't swim. Anyway, I was scared that he was going to fall in. Sure enough, the neighbor kid fell overboard. My son dived in to help him. I was stuck on the shore, just watching this go on right in front of my eyes.

"Then the next thing I knew, the neighbor climbed back into the canoe! But my son was thrashing around in the water and calling for me to come out and save him. I couldn't. I was frozen in my tracks. Even though he wasn't more than one hundred feet from the shore, I couldn't move to save him. In my dream I heard him screaming, 'Daddy! Daddy!' but I just stood there crying," David recounted.

"Is that how your dream ends?" I inquired.

"No," he replied. "After he started to sink into the lake, it was like my dream went to a split screen or something because then I saw him as he dropped slowly underwater. I saw his face like it was right up next to mine. I saw him try to breathe underwater until finally he drifted lifelessly to rest at the muddy bottom of the lake," David said quietly.

He went on to explain how that ended his dream. He woke up right when his son drowned at the bottom of the lake. David said he was trembling when he awoke, and he had sweated through his pajamas. He couldn't stop himself from checking on his son, who was sleeping in the next room.

"And you found him asleep in his room?" I inquired.

"Yes," he replied. "Brandon was there. So I put it out of my mind as best I could and forced myself to go back to bed."

"Okay, I'm following you, David, but these types of dreams are not particularly unusual for parents. We're always worried about our kids being hurt, and these worries often filter through into our dreams," I said.

"I know, I know," he said impatiently. "I understand the logic of that, but what I'm about to tell you, I have no explanation for." Continuing, the pastor said, "The following day, I got this phone call that shook me up even more than the dream had. The call was from the youth pastor who works for me as a camp counselor at our summer retreat up in the Sequoias. He called in a panic to apologize for some trouble at the camp. He told me that the previous night, two boys had sneaked out of their cabins for a moonlit raft ride on the lake. When their raft deflated, the boys—neither wearing a life vest—spilled into the lake. Apparently another counselor heard their cries for help and summoned rescuers, who were able to rescue the boys.

"My camp counselor told me that both boys were checked out by the emergency room doctor and released at about one A.M. The doctor said they were both okay, but one kid, Mike, had swallowed a lot of water and probably came about as close to drowning as you can come and still walk away from it."

David paused and gave me the opportunity to ask whether he had known either of the boys.

"That's what's so strange," he replied. "Out of a hundred campers, it turned out that the boy who nearly drowned is our next-door neighbor. He's the same kid I saw in my dream—my son's best friend. In fact, my boy had invited him to go to this camp because his family is not religious and we thought it would be a good opportunity for him to be around some Christian kids. My son ended up not being able to go because he had the flu, so the neighbor kid went with a couple of other kids they all knew.

"So, the following day, I went next door to visit the parents of the boy. I figured that at least I owed them an apology since I was the one who suggested they let their son attend the camp. And besides, I'm the senior pastor and am ultimately responsible for the church and its camp activities."

"And how did that conversation go?" I asked.

"Well, it was odd. They were very understanding about what had happened. Dale, the young man's father, even joked that we probably wouldn't see his son for about thirty years because that's when his restriction would be over. Denise, his mom, seemed troubled and wanted to know if she could ask a spiritual question."

"And what did she ask you?" I said.

"Well, she asked me if I believed in premonitions or extrasensory perception."

"And you said . . ."

"I said, no, I didn't think people could read other people's minds. Then I asked her why she wanted to know.

"She said that she had some kind of nightmare involving her son while he was away at the camp. She couldn't really recall anything about the dream, but she knew that whatever it was, it really scared her. The oddest thing was that she said she was so upset that she didn't even try to go back to sleep. Instead she got up and watched *The Tonight Show*," he recounted.

I spent the next fifteen seconds trying to figure out why David would think that watching *The Tonight Show* after a nightmare was particularly odd, and then it struck me. "So what you're saying is that you think your neighbor had a nightmare at eleven-twenty-three P.M., which was the time you awakened from yours," I said.

"That's the sixty-four-thousand-dollar question. Have you ever heard of dreams doing this, and could she have been right about its being a premonition?" he asked.

"Yes, I have heard of these types of simultaneous dreams, but they usually involve close family members," I replied. "Back in the Vietnam War years, there were several cases of family members living in different states awakening from dreams at the same time that a family member had been killed. I don't remember the statistics, but I think I recall the dates and times checked out with the military and were found to coincide with the dates and times of the deaths."

As if registering the words I was speaking for the first time, I said, "As long as we're venturing down that trail, Pastor, do you have any idea what time the neighbor boy and his friend fell into the lake?"

"I knew you would ask that, Doctor," he responded almost proudly. "Get this! I got a copy of the paramedic's report for insurance reasons, and it lists the time the call was received at exactly eleven-thirty-three P.M. So, the closest we can figure is that the boys were in the water at approximately the same time we were both having our dreams."

Epilogue

From my years as a detective, I recall a term that fits a situation like this. The term was a *preponderance of evidence*. To the legal system, a preponderance of evidence means even though you didn't have an eyewitness to place the suspect at the crime scene, there was other overwhelming evidence that did. Often it was a combination of fingerprints, DNA, motive, and opportunity that came together to provide a clear verdict. The concept applies as neatly in dream science as it did in police science. When there's a preponderance of evidence that a dream has divine elements, any reasonable and prudent person would accept the finding.

Of all dream types I've documented, dreams such as the one revealed by this pastor are perhaps the most rare. *Simultaneous dreams*—that is, similar dreams received by one or more persons at nearly or exactly the same time—are rare occurrences. Perhaps even more rare are simultaneous dreams that touch both a Christian and a non-Christian. When this phenomenon takes place, it should be regarded as a divine dream; therefore, the Christian should seek God's leading, especially in regard to the non-Christian dreamer. I generally come away from these experiences with a sense that the dream was God's way of encouraging the Christian to witness to the non-Christian.

As a final thought, I suggested that the pastor examine his dream from the perspective that it could have been a warning. Whether divine or not, it would be imprudent to discount a warning. I also suggested the pastor examine safety policies to see if this type of incident could be prevented in the future.

CASE NOTES:

The Black Widows' Deadly Web

NAME: Lauren
AGE: 31
OCCUPATION: Legal secretary
MARITAL STATUS: Separated from husband, 2 children
(ages 6 and 4)

I had just completed a lengthy dream interview as a guest on a Christian radio station when the show's producer asked if I would take a phone call from an emotional caller who was unable to get through during the program. Agreeing, I excused myself and went into another studio where the producer handed me the phone.

The woman identified herself as Lauren and told me that she had spent the previous two hours alternating between anguish and hope. On the one hand, she wanted to get through to talk about a horrible recurring nightmare she'd been having. On the other, she believed that dream interpretation was for weak-minded people who have to depend on psychology for help instead of God.

"I agree with part of your position, Lauren," I replied. "Far too many people do depend on psychology, and far too few people depend on God." Continuing, I said, "Lauren, you didn't call me to tell me what we both already know. The producer told me that you've been having a disturbing dream. Would you like me to help you with it if I can?"

Lauren quietly and reluctantly replied, "Yes."

Assuring her that she could stop at any time, I said, "Let's start with the dream only. Don't tell me anything about your personal life that might interfere with how I interpret your dream. Deal?"

"Deal," Lauren replied.

"All right then, I'm going to ask you a few questions, and then I'll ask you to tell me about your dream. Try to put yourself in the same mood and emotion that you feel when you are having this dream. If I interrupt you to ask you a question, don't derail yourself by wondering why I'm asking it or by thinking too much about the answer. Just tell me the first thing that comes to mind and then pick up right where you left off. Are you ready?" I asked.

"Ready," came her reply.

"How often do you have this dream, and when did it start, Lauren?" I inquired.

"I have the dream at least once a week, and I started having it about three months ago."

"How do you feel during and right after you awaken from your dream?" I questioned.

Hesitating, she replied, "I am a complete and emotional wreck. I wake up trembling and in a cold sweat. Sometimes I'm crying, and at other times I'm too angry and scared to cry."

"I understand. So tell me what you remember of your dreams," I encouraged her.

Lauren took a deep breath and began, "The dream takes place in my home . . . that is, my and my husband's house. I'm always asleep in my bed when I hear noises coming from my son's bedroom. He's six years old. I get out of bed and walk slowly and quietly to the door of his room, but the door is locked. I know he's still asleep, but I keep hearing these strange noises coming from the heating and air-conditioning vents in his room. I look up, and there are hundreds of large spiders crawling through the vents from outside his room to the inside. Even though in my dream I'm physically outside his room and his door is closed, I can tell that the spiders are scurrying through the air vents in a straight line toward him as he's sleeping in his bed.

"Finally I'm able to break the door down, and as I burst into his room, I can see that the spiders have crawled up onto his bed. Some of them have formed a circle around him as if to keep me back while the others have entered his head through his eyes and ears. He just looks frightened, and his eyes are helplessly staring at me like he's waiting for me to rescue him. But I can't even move. I'm paralyzed and helpless with fear.

"We stare at each other while the spiders weave and envelop him in a web until he can't see or hear me any longer. Then the web they've woven begins to suffocate my son. I'm still standing frozen in fear at his doorway while he struggles to breathe, but it's hopeless. I awaken from my nightmare just as he is gasping for his last breath," she concluded, her voice trailing off as if reliving the dream for the first time.

In the span of about three minutes, Lauren's recounting of her dreadful recurring nightmare had revealed volumes about what was going on in her life. Unbeknownst to Lauren, she probably revealed more through describing the dream than she cared to admit.

"When did you separate from or divorce your husband?" I inquired.

"How did you know I was separated from my husband?" she asked in a surprised tone.

"I'll tell you in a minute, but I'm guessing that you are separated and not divorced. Do you mind me asking which?" I said.

"We're temporarily separated," she stated.

"And your dream suggests you live alone in your home with at least one child," I continued.

"Correct," she replied, still sounding surprised. "As I said, my husband and I are going through a trial separation. He moved out about seven months ago."

"So your current situation is that you and your husband are not planning on getting back together, you've filed for divorce, and you have joint custody of your child or children?" I asked.

"Absolutely not!" she snapped. "We still talk, and I think there is a fair chance we'll get back together."

"I stand corrected," I said. "Let me tell you why I made that assumption. You began your dream by saying that it takes place in your home. Then you corrected yourself and said it takes place in your and your husband's house. You see, Lauren, women tend to use the word *house* when it's just a place to live, but *home* when it's a place where a family resides. That statement alone pointed to the likelihood of separation or divorce."

"I called to discuss my dream, not my marriage. So if you don't mind, can you tell me what the spiders mean? I'm wondering if God is sending me a warning about my son's safety. Is that possible?" she inquired.

Carefully measuring my words, I replied, "Lauren, I don't know if your dream is divinely inspired, but that may come out as we make some sense of your dream. Once you fully understand it, then you'll be in a much better position to determine if it's of God or just your subconscious.

"These spiders in your dream . . . I need to know a little more about them. Do you know what kind of spiders they are?" I questioned.

Without hesitation, Lauren replied, "They're black widows, but they're much larger than normal black widow spiders. They're at least as big as a hand."

"That's significant, Lauren. Because they're black widow spiders, your dream is suggesting something that is directly connected to your life. First things first, Lauren. The black widow spiders represent a female dream archetype, that is, a dream symbol for powerful and sinister women. That means we can start by assuming your dream revolves around a woman whom you see as larger than life and potentially dangerous. Are you with me?" I asked.

"Yes, I'm with you, but why are they in the air vents in my son's room, and why do they crawl into his eyes and ears and wrap their web around his face?" she asked with a hint of panic in her voice.

"Lauren, the fact that they are crawling through the air vents is very significant. Air is a dream symbol that relates to sustaining life, but it differs from food and water in that you can't detect it with your senses. Therefore, it can turn harmful and even poisonous without your knowing it. Let's start to stack these first dream symbols so we can follow the trail. We're looking for some female in your life who is definitely not on your side. You see her as dangerous and sneaky in that she seems to have access to your child without your even knowing it. Ready to handle a little more?" I inquired.

"Yes," Lauren replied, "but this is getting a little uncomfortable."

"That's actually a good sign, Lauren," I assured her. Pressing on, I said, "The reason the spiders are coming through the air vents is that you probably feel that you have protected your son in all the ways you normally can protect a child. But the air vents are unexpected; only someone who is sneaky would creep into his life through the air vents.

"The spiders are surrounding and then entering your son through his eyes and ears because you are afraid that this person is filling his head with lies or evil thoughts. Think of some female in his world who you think is playing mind games with him. Are you getting a mental image of someone?" I asked.

There was silence on the other end of the phone followed by a deep breath. Then Lauren spoke: "You're right. There is a woman in my son's life. I'm very much afraid of what she is doing and saying about me behind my back to my son. And she happens to be my husband's little friend. She is not a Christian, and I can tell by the way my son comes home after weekend visits that his head has been filled with anti-Mom and anti-Christian garbage."

"Lauren, here's what I think your dream is telling you. Your dream is about a woman who is somehow connected to your son. You see her as aggressive, sneaky, and potentially deadly. Your dream reveals that you feel powerless to stop this woman, which means she is not someone who respects you or your wishes. Based on that, it wouldn't shock me if this woman is the one you described as a friend of your husband. Because your son is the focal point, a probable angle is that you suspect she's trying to turn your son against you."

I could hear nothing on the other end of the phone, and for a moment I wondered if she had hung up. "I'm starting to get the picture," she said finally. "So what you're saying, Doctor, is that my entire dream is telling me to pay attention to this woman who is sabotaging me with my own child."

"That's just one message I take away from your dream," I cautioned. "I don't want to discount that one at all, but there is a second theme that you might at least want to acknowledge."

"What's that?" she inquired.

"I'm hesitant to bring it up because of some things you've said about your marital situation. I understand you are temporarily separated and are holding hopes of getting back together. For your sake, and if it is God's will, I pray that happens, but there's a second connotation to the black widows. Lauren, are you aware of the term *denial?*" I asked cautiously.

"Yes, if you mean in the context of when you know something deep inside, but you don't want to think about it or admit it," she replied.

"Exactly," I answered. "I suspect your dream is trying to break through your denial regarding your husband and marriage. Black widow spiders in dreams can play a dual role. It's clear from your dream that the first role is that the spider is spinning a web of deceit in your son's mind. The second role of the black widow is that of a sexual predator. What do you know of a black widow's mating habits, Lauren?"

"Not that I study these things, but I think I saw a documentary on how she attracts the male spider so she can mate with it. Then unless I'm mistaken, she kills the male spider," she answered. "Are you saying you think this woman is going to kill my husband?"

"You took too large a leap," I replied. "I'm saying that another way of interpreting the black widows in your dream is that at least subconsciously, you suspect this woman is more than just your husband's friend. You may not allow yourself to go there during your waking hours, but you can't control your subconscious while you are asleep. Your dream suggests you have unconscious, or repressed, suspicions about this relationship, and your subconscious is trying to force you out of denial."

Lauren didn't answer immediately. Then slowly she asked, "Assuming that I accept what you are saying as the truth, what is my next step?"

"First, I respect what you just said. None of us like to hear bad news—especially when we've worked so hard to deny or repress it," I said. "I think the important thing to understand now is the origin of your dream. The two sources of dreams are self-initiated and God-initiated. We know that self-initiated dreams come from situations in the past and present. As for God-initiated dreams, Scripture doesn't allow for any being to have access to our dreams except God. So in respect to your recurring nightmare, the source is either your anxiety about your marriage and this woman, or God, in which case He is sending you these dreams to get you to take action."

"So, how do I know which type of dream this is?" she inquired.

"That's the tough question," I replied. "The first thing is to avoid any knee-jerk reactions. Test the spirit—the sense you have of your dream—by seeking counsel from your pastor, your elders, and one or two smart and spiritually minded people you trust. Prayerfully submit the situation to God, and ask Him for guidance and wisdom as to what to do next. It's fair to ask Him to clarify if the dream is from Him by sending you a sign or giving you peace of mind about a certain solution. My experience is that self-initiated, anxiety-driven dreams tend to go away once you expose them to the light of day. The process of breaking through our own denial seems to send a signal to the subconscious that we are finally tuned in."

"What about dreams from God?" she asked. "If I do nothing, do I get zapped by a lightning bolt?"

"I don't see that happening much, but just to be on the safe side, you may want to wear rubber-soled shoes and stay clear of puddles," I joked. "But seriously, if yours was a God-initiated dream, then prayerfully waiting and watching for a short—emphasis on the word *short*—period of time is the recommended course. In these situations I've had people tell me they get hit with a wide range of feelings, from sort of uneasy to downright uncomfortable. Whereas once they were quite satisfied to hang out in denial and do nothing, all of a sudden waiting starts to feel like the worst thing. That can be read as confirmation of a God-initiated dream.

"Or in some cases, I've seen God initiate dreams that were confirmed with the return of the exact, or nearly exact, nightmare. One patient jokingly referred to this as 'Remedial Dreaming 101' because it reminded him of school and having to sit through the same lecture a second time because he wasn't paying attention the first time."

I concluded by asking Lauren if she would call me back in one week to let me know what, if any, changes had occurred in her nightmares.

CHECK MY SOURCES

True to her word, Lauren called my office exactly one week after our conversation. She stated she had taken my advice and elected to sit tight and not take any action. She mused, "I'd waited seven months, so what was another week?"

During the week, she had prayed for clarity and spoken with her pastor and church elders, who also prayed and made several suggestions. First, they supported her that the dream *could* very well have been God's way of warning her about her son's mental well-being, and they urged her to take steps to protect him. They even suggested a restraining order to keep the girlfriend away from Lauren's son. Although she initially had not entered these meetings seeking direction in her marriage, they offered the idea that her husband might be having an affair and suggested she confront him directly.

Lauren filed a temporary restraining order to keep the girlfriend away from her son, but discounted the advice about an affair being grounds for divorce. Lauren seemed unprepared to deal with confronting her husband and the likely outcome that would come with hearing the truth.

CASE NOTES:

A Travel Advisory

NAME: Grace
AGE: 39
OCCUPATION: Nurse
MARITAL STATUS: Married 12 years, with 1 son (age 10)

From experience I've found that nurses, irrespective of gender, tend to have vivid and often frightening dreams. The only plausible explanation is that they work in a high-stress profession where they see more than their share of pain and suffering.

To this point, no matter the origin, we know that dreams are always connected to our waking lives. When we experience situations that produce overwhelming negative emotions such as fear, hatred, dread, trauma, grief, and anxiety, and these feelings are unresolved, they nearly always show up in our dreams. That is the mind's way of prompting us out of denial and into a place where we can identify, examine and, it is hoped, resolve the cause of that emotion.

No one could deny that hospital employees likely see more emotionally troubling images in one day than most people see in a year. Perhaps it was for that reason that when Grace scheduled an appointment, I presupposed her dream would likely be attributed to job stress and not to a mother's intuition or divine intervention.

In our first session, Grace described herself as "somewhere between an atheist and an agnostic." She had been raised in the Four Square Church in

Oklahoma. After her parents passed away, Grace decided she had had enough of church. Her reasoning was that religion was a personal issue and that if she chose to become spiritual once again, she could do it without ever having to return to organized religion. "Religion," she stated, "can be a great thing, but church can be a colossal waste of time and money that works best for weak-minded people. No offense," she added, referring to my background.

"None taken," I responded as weak-mindedly as I could.

Although I had a suspicion that Grace at least wondered if God was connected to her dream, I decided to leave that alone for now. Taking a non-confrontational route, I started the interview: "So, tell me a bit about the dreams you've been having."

Leaning forward and becoming slightly tense, Grace replied, "I've had a series of dreams over a period of four consecutive nights that I think are connected."

If Grace's dreams were in fact connected to one another, they would represent a rare dream phenomenon I call *serial dreams*. I refer to them this way because they appear consecutively, one night after the other, undeniably connected by at least one common theme or thread. Sometimes they appear as a made-for-television movie that has been broken into two or more parts. Each consecutive dream picks up where the last dream stopped. It's as if at the end of the previous dream, the mind placed a commercial break reading: *tune in tomorrow night for the continuing drama.* In these dreams, much like a *Matlock, ER,* or *CSI* episode, the dreamer will tune in each night and recognize the cast, characters, set, and plot from the previous show. Even though the story line might have changed slightly, each subsequent dream is substantively connected to the previous one.

Eager to hear Grace's serial dream, I asked, "How long ago did you experience the first dream and for how many nights did it continue?"

"The first dream came about ten days ago, and I've had three similar dreams in a row. Then they stopped," she replied.

"Why don't you start with what we'll call episode number one and tell me about it?" I asked. "But before you do, were any of these dreams of a variety that would cause you to awaken crying?"

Grace's eyes widened in surprise as she responded, "Yes! I woke up crying, no, actually sobbing after all three. My poor husband thought I'd lost my mind. I mean, here I am three nights in a row waking up in the middle of the night, sobbing my eyes out."

"I'm sure that was tough for him as well," I consoled her. "Can you pinpoint the emotion that drives you to tears in your dreams?"

"Absolutely!" she said. "I was grief stricken! After each dream, for three nights in a row, I awakened in tears with this overwhelming sense of grief that haunted me throughout my day."

"Can you compare the sense of grief you felt in your dreams to any other grief you've experienced in life?" I asked.

Thinking for a moment, Grace replied, "The closest I can come was when my father died. I mourned for a long time, and that felt like the same grief I felt following my dreams."

"Thanks, Grace, that helps," I said. "Why don't you tell me about the first dream?"

Grace began recounting her first dream slowly: "In my first dream, I was sitting in my van in the parking lot of my son's school. I was there early. Knowing that I had about a half hour to kill, I began taking pictures of the kids while they were playing on the playground. I'm not really sure why I was taking pictures, but I knew that I needed to get a snapshot of each and every one of them. I also realized that it really bothered me that the lighting wasn't just perfect because I needed these pictures to come out right.

"Then I noticed that it was getting terribly dark, and the sky looked as if it was going to open up and pour rain at any second. It made me feel rushed and nervous that I had to get those pictures taken quickly. Then the bell rang, and all the kids ran away from where I was taking their pictures. They were all gone from the playground for about a minute, but then they reappeared in a straight line and were walking toward some kind of monument that was planted in the middle of the playground," she continued. "In real life, there is no monument at their school."

I asked her to describe the monument for me.

"I can't in much detail," she replied. "All I can recall is that it reminded me of one of those historical landmark monuments they put up around old buildings or at scenic places along the roadway. You know the ones. They're cement or granite and have a bronze plaque with some inscription. Oh, and in my dream I saw an empty vase . . . you know . . . a flower vase on the ground next to the monument, but it was empty. That's all I recall about my first dream, except for the uncontrollable sadness and grief I felt when I awakened."

"Okay," I said while giving her a moment to collect her thoughts. "Let's take a look at your second dream."

"In my second dream, I picked up where I was watching all the kids lined up, single file, on the playground. I didn't have a camera this time. The skies had actually gotten darker, and I could tell that a giant storm was brewing. Then the kids all looked at me for an instant, as though I had called to them or something. Then they started filing one by one past the monument," she recalled. "But the part that tears me up the most is that they were all crying as they walked past the monument. Then I woke up."

I asked her if she had a sense of what the kids were doing as they walked past the monument, but she said she really didn't know. She did know that it was sad, and that it made her cry in her dream and when she awakened too. It was time to hear her third dream.

"In my third dream," Grace said, "I was driving in my van to pick up my son after school. It was odd because the weather was really nice when I left home, but as soon as I got near school, the sky turned almost pitch-black, like it had in my two previous dreams. Then it started raining sheets of water, and I started to panic that the weather was so bad that the teachers wouldn't dismiss the kids. Just about the time I pulled into the parking lot of his school, there were lightning strikes all around. I thought it was strange because the lightning was striking the playground all around that monument. It was the same monument that was in my other dreams, only this time the vase had one flower in it."

"Can you discern the type or color of flower in the vase?" I asked.

Closing her eyes as if to force herself to see it in her mind, she said with surprise, "Oh, my goodness, yes! I do remember what kind of flower was in the vase. It was a pink carnation!"

"What takes place next?" I asked.

"Then all of the kids were standing at the side of the field, where they always wait for their parents to pick them up," she recalled. "But it was still pouring rain, and I was thinking they were crazy to have the kids standing out in the lightning and rain like that. Then as I was pulling up toward the pickup area, I noticed that there was suddenly a long line of parents in their cars ahead of me. But they weren't stopping to pick up their children; they were just driving slowly past all the kids. As I finally got my turn at the pickup point, I could see my son in the crowd of kids. He was crying and reaching his arms out to me. We made eye contact, but I couldn't stop my car. I tried to put on the brakes, but the pedal went all the way to the floor. I couldn't even slow down because my car kept moving past him in line with all the other cars.

"That's when I woke up, and I was really a mess. I mean, I had this mental image of my son stuck on the field in floods of rain with lightning all around, and he kept crying and reaching out for me as I drove by," she concluded while reaching into her purse for a tissue.

"I'm sorry, Grace," I said. "Dream or not, that is quite a disturbing image. Let's move on to the fourth episode dream. It occurred the very next night?" I asked.

"Yes," she replied. "But it didn't take place at my son's school, even though I know it was still connected to the three previous dreams."

"Tell me about it, please."

"In this dream, I was working at the hospital, but I wasn't working in my usual unit," she said. "Instead of being on the general medical floor, I was working in the emergency room."

"Do you ever work in the ER?" I asked.

"No, never. I'm not certified to work there. Even if I were, I couldn't take it," she replied. "Especially when kids come in. Anyway, we were working on a woman who'd been brought in after a horrible car accident, and I recognized her as a mom of one of the kids in my son's class. I don't know her name, but I had met her at some back-to-school night or other school function. She just kept telling me that *she was sorry.* That's all she said, over and over again. *She was sorry. She was so sorry.* Then I noticed that I was holding her hand and that she was squeezing mine back. Then it went limp, and she was dead."

"You said you knew your fourth dream was connected to the previous ones. Was the only connection that it involved a parent of one of your son's classmates?" I asked.

"Oh, no," she replied. "There's more that ties them all together. After the mother died, I heard a loud noise coming from outside. I walked to the double glass doors of the emergency room and stood watching the rain pouring down. Then just like at school, a long line of cars being driven by all the parents came filing slowly past the doors of the ER. It was still pouring rain and lightning was striking everywhere, but I could still make out the image of one parent and one child in each car. I kept staring, trying to figure out why all these parents were driving in a slow, straight line by the hospital when I saw—" She stopped to regain her composure. "I saw myself driving my car. I was following right behind one car, and another car was right behind me. But I was alone. I was the only parent who didn't have her child with her."

I gave Grace a moment to collect her thoughts before asking, "Is there anything else you remember about that dream prior to your awakening?"

Drawing in a slow, deep breath, Grace continued, "I was standing there, staring out the door of the ER at myself in the car. Then the *me* in my car looked right at the *me* in the hospital, and we locked eyes for about a minute. We were both crying, but neither of us said anything. I knew, though, that something tragic had happened to her.

"And I noticed one more thing," she added. "There was a pink carnation on the dashboard of my car as I drove slowly by the doors of the ER. That's when I realized that whatever was going on was all related to my son. I woke myself up crying."

"You were correct, Grace," I said. "This is one of the most unusual assemblages of dreams and symbols I've encountered, but I'm sure we can get a handle on their meaning."

The secret to solving serial dreams is to draw out the common dream symbols that connect each dream. I had several valuable pieces of the puzzle to work with, so I wanted to get started. From my notes, I would track the prominent dream symbols from dream to dream, starting with the first episode. Grace was at her child's school, and all the kids were lined up single file.

Turning to Grace, I asked, "What does it mean to you when you see the kids lined up single file?"

"It means they are getting ready to go somewhere," she replied.

Nodding my head in agreement, I said, "That's what I get as well. Let's see if this ties into the next dream symbol you gave me, which was your taking pictures of the kids. You said that you didn't know why you were taking pictures of them, but that you felt a sense of urgency to do so. As a dream symbol, urgently taking pictures of people denotes a fear that they are going away and you won't see them again. Think of it like going on vacation to somewhere special. You get a sense that you must take as many pictures as possible before you leave so that you'll have something to remember the vacation by. This is driven by the thought that you may never see that place again.

"It's the same with pictures of people. Based on the first two symbols, I think we have a match. You are projecting that one or more of the kids in your child's school are going somewhere and you are afraid you will not see them again. You also said that the skies were 'terribly dark' and it looked like rain. Storms approaching in dreams nearly always represent an anxiety over some pending problem, as in trouble on the horizon.

"The next significant symbol was the monument that appeared on the playground at your son's school. You described the monument as being made out of cement or granite and having a bronze plaque with an unknown inscription," I said, pausing to think. "This one can go one of two ways, and it will get clearer as we unravel the other symbols. For now, let's suppose that we are dealing with a cemetery headstone or possibly a government-type monument marker. I lean toward a government image because you called it a monument, but we can't discount a headstone because we've established your nervousness over someone going away and never seeing the person again. For now, let's just wait and see.

"Your next dream symbol was an empty vase on the ground next to the monument. In these types of symbols, it isn't always what's *there*, but what's *not* there that is most important. In this case, what are missing are flowers. By nearly all dream interpretation standards, flowers represent something to do with life; therefore, the absence of flowers denotes death," I said while stopping a moment so Grace could gather it all in.

Forging ahead, I said, "Now let's tie the first dream's symbols and meanings together to give us a sense of where we are before we move into your second dream. We've got the kids lined up getting ready to go somewhere. Stormy skies representing trouble on the horizon. We've got you taking pictures of someone you fear you'll never see again. We've got a possible cemetery grave marker or government monument. And finally we've got flowers missing from a vase, which tells us you are anticipating someone dying. With me so far?" I asked with a smile.

She nodded before I resumed.

"Moving on to your second dream, we see the children and playground theme again, but a significant difference is that the students on the playground all looked at you for a moment and then began filing, one by one, past the monument," I said.

"Grace, let me pose the question to you. What is it a sign of when kids look you in the eye?" I asked.

"I don't know . . . I guess it's a sign of respect or they're connecting with you," she replied.

"Exactly," I agreed. "Lock in on the word *respect*, and tell me what you see when a group of people look at you as they file, one by one, past a monument?"

"Let's see," she said as she silently mouthed the word *respect* again and again until she looked straight into my eyes. "They're paying their respects to me. It's like the monument is a gravestone and the kids are paying their last respects."

"Very nice reasoning, Grace," I encouraged her. "I think you are right on target.

"Now let's say the monument is just that and not a gravestone. If it's a monument, Grace, what does the image of the kids walking single file past it do for you?" I asked.

Squinting her eyes and biting the inside of her lip, Grace replied, "I get an image of kids at a museum or somewhere like that."

"Ah, yes," I replied. "That's excellent. I can see the connection.

"Next, you told me that the skies were growing even darker than in your previous night's dream recollection. That tells us that the problem you are anticipating is even larger than you had originally braced for. Although we're starting to get a picture of what you were bracing yourself for, let's not tackle it until we've looked at some additional symbols," I cautioned.

"Just store those symbols in the back of your mind for a moment while we decipher your third of four dreams," I said. "I'm particularly interested in the image of good weather as you are going to pick up your son at school. But once at school, the weather turns dark and stormy. This narrows the serious problem on the horizon to something related to school and not to home, family, or friends.

"Also, your vase symbol reappeared in this dream with a significant change, Grace. What was it?" I asked.

"There's a flower in it this time," she replied.

"Precisely, and when you close your eyes and envision a vase with one flower in it, what does that mean to you?"

Almost a minute passed as Grace searched her visual memory for an image. Finally she said, "It reminds me of a cemetery and how each gravestone has a vase next to it. In fact, I was visiting my mom's grave a short time ago, and I was surprised to see that someone had left a flower in her vase."

"What kind of flower was it?" I inquired.

"It was actually a lovely carnation," she replied. "I thought it was touching that someone at the cemetery or a visitor cared enough to leave a flower. I'm the only one who visits her grave, so I haven't the foggiest idea who might have left it."

"Interesting," I commented. "Next, you told me that your son and all the children were standing in the pouring rain, with lightning flashing all around, and you thought it was crazy that the teachers were letting the kids go outside in that weather," I recalled. "The significant symbol here is your thought that the teachers must be crazy for putting the kids in jeopardy. Lock in on the word *jeopardy.*

"Then you told me that you were suddenly in a long line of cars being driven by the other parents," I reminded her. "As it was your turn to pick up your son, you couldn't stop your car. He started crying and reaching out while you had to helplessly drive by and leave him at school. Question for you, Grace."

"What's that?" she replied.

"What do you see when I describe a long line of single-file cars traveling slowly in the same direction?" I asked.

Without hesitation, she replied, "I see a funeral procession."

"Precisely," I affirmed. "Good work. Now let's reason why your son couldn't get into your car. In your dream, all we know is that he was upset and crying, and you were upset and crying because you couldn't reach each other. If we were taking a stab at trying to understand what's going on in your world that's driving this dream so far, I'd start to look at your anxiety over taking him or letting him go somewhere by car. Probably because you are afraid something bad might happen.

"Either way, I think we're on the right trail. Shall we look at the fourth installment of your serial dream?" I said without waiting for an answer.

"In your final dream, you are working in the ER at the hospital instead of on your usual floor. This is your dream's way of telling you that you are nervous about a potential emergency, but more important that you are nervous about something major you don't think you can handle emotionally," I explained.

"Your next symbol is that you are treating a mom whom you recognize as the mother of one of your son's classmates. Correct?" I asked.

"Yes," she replied.

"She had been in a terrible car accident, and you were holding her hand as she looked up to you and told you she was very sorry."

Interrupting, Grace added, "But she never said what she was sorry for."

"It's true that she didn't say the words, but your dream symbols tell us what she's referring to. Apologizing to you for a car accident she's had does not make sense, so we need to assume she's apologizing for something she's done to you in her accident," I answered.

"Then what is it in my dream that explains what she's sorry for?" Grace asked impatiently.

"Your next dream symbol clears that up," I replied. "You looked out the ER doors and saw that it was still dark and rainy, and lightning was still striking. That tells us that you were still expecting big trouble. Next, you saw a funeral procession image of cars passing by the ER doors. You noticed that each car had both a parent and a child inside. Then you recognized your car as it passed the door. You saw yourself driving, but your son was not in the car. And then finally the symbol of the pink carnation reappeared, only this time it was out of the vase and on the dashboard of your car."

Taking a deep breath as if to ease some of the tension we were both feeling, I continued, "Here's what I think your collective dreams are telling you. I think you have recently experienced, or are currently experiencing, a significant amount of anxiety about your son. Because cars in a funeral procession or a car that your son can't get into is a theme in your serial dreams, I believe your anxiety involves your son taking a trip. Because a central theme is his school, you seem to be saying that you are frightened about him taking a school trip. A trip that the storm clouds in your dreams tell us you see as risky and potentially deadly.

"The part that isn't clear to me is that pesky dream symbol of the monument that keeps wanting to turn into a cemetery grave marker," I said, tilting my head to the side as if that would somehow help. "By any chance is your son's class planning a trip somewhere that you're nervous about?"

Grace stared motionlessly at me about thirty seconds. Finally, shaking her head slowly, she said, "How did you get that out of my dreams? I never connected it. Every year, his school takes the fifth graders on an overnight field trip to the state capital. The trip is in two weeks. Most other years they've had buses to take the kids. But this year they didn't have it in the budget so they asked for parent volunteers. I told them I couldn't do it because of my work, but I'm really nervous about him getting in the car with someone I don't know. I mean, it's a four-hour trip each way, it's always raining this time of year, and part of the trip is over the mountain. I've been arguing with my husband, who says I shouldn't be so protective, but I can't shake this feeling that it's a big mistake to let him go."

"Then the monument is actually two things," I said, feeling just a little bit self-satisfied. "It's a government monument representing the field trip to the state capital first, but then it transforms into a gravestone following the accident. It is fascinating how you did that in your dreams, Grace."

"I follow what you're saying now. So, what do I do? Either I ignore the dreams and let him go, or I admit that I'm superstitious and hold him back," she said with a tone of desperation in her voice.

"There are three ways you can account for these dreams," I said. "The first is that they are nonsense and should be dispatched like a used tissue. The second is that you are receiving what I call a mother's intuition, in which case you'd be foolish to discount it. The third is that God is sending you a series of warning dreams in an attempt to get your attention. I know you struggle with spiritual issues, but at least consider that God might be warning you about an impending tragedy."

Sitting back half-disgustedly into the folds of the couch, she replied, "What would you do if you were me? I mean, I refuse to believe that God tosses dreams around like dog snacks to weak-minded people who snap them up . . . Oh, I'm sorry again about the weak-minded implication," she said sheepishly.

"Ouch," I replied. "But I think you have three things to consider. If you're wrong and the dreams are from God, then you've made a huge mistake. If it's a mother's intuition, then you're foolish not to trust your instincts. And if you think four interconnected dreams are just nonsense and superstition, then you should let your son go.

"Look, Grace," I continued. "The point of this is not to witness to you, but I can't recall a serial dream, especially as vivid and consecutively pieced together for four nights like yours is, that *did not* appear to have divine roots. If he were my son, I would take the time off and drive him myself. Otherwise, I wouldn't let him go. Do me a favor, won't you?" I asked. "Call me and let me know how everything turns out. Until then, I'll be praying for you," I said with a smile.

"Thanks!" she replied. "I guess prayer wouldn't hurt."

EPILOGUE

I've encountered only a handful of serial dreams over the years. In each case, the dreamer was a spiritual person with relatively little difficulty attributing the dreams to divine intervention. Because Grace claimed to be wandering spiritually, it made me wonder if she were somewhat more open to God than she let on. You can never discount that God might be using her dreams, and me, to draw her closer to Him.

About three weeks later, Grace called me to say that, discretion being the better part of valor, she had chosen to take time off from work to drive her son and several classmates to the state capital. She laughingly joked that I'd be relieved to learn that God didn't cause any accidents or even near misses.

She did, however, report something odd. She said she had just started down the steep mountain highway toward the state capital when she passed a historical monument turnout in the highway. As she glanced over at the granite marker, she felt a strange tingling sensation that started in her temples and traveled down her neck and through her arms. The sensation caused her to hyperventilate momentarily as though she were having an anxiety attack. Being a nurse, Grace passed it off as a combination of altitude and a car full of hyper students.

She told me that she had to tell me because she knew I'd immediately jump to the conclusion that the historical monument was likely the place where the accident would have taken place had God not warned me. I jokingly told her that was the last thing on my mind, but that I'd be happy to pray about it.

Evangelizing is a delicate situation and one that necessitates observing God's timing and leading. Although I didn't jump on the opportunity to tell Grace that there was no doubt in my mind that God had sent her a message, I know it was clear to her exactly where I stood.

CASE NOTES:

The Goose That Laid a Golden Egg

NAME: Wes
AGE: 36
OCCUPATION: VP marketing/software field
MARITAL STATUS: Married, with 2 children

A constant source of frustration for any talk-radio "shrink" comes in finding the balance between entertainment and psychology. I acquiesced to blurring that balance once a week when we held the Top 10 Bizarre Dreams Contest featuring lovely parting gifts for runners-up, while the winner received something virtually worthless—one of my parenting books. Ah, if my professors could see me now, wouldn't they be proud? As far as entertainment value goes, however, listening to people's dreams is a big ratings hit.

"Next up we've got Wes in Los Angeles. Ah, and looking at my call screen, I see that Wes wants to talk about fruit trees. How appropriate, and welcome to the program, Wes."

"Hi, Doctor," Wes greeted me. "Your screener only got part of it right. My dream involves me *planting* fruit trees," he corrected.

"*Planting* fruit trees?" I repeated. "Although planting fruit trees does sound interesting, Wes, I must remind you that you're up against the woman who dreamed she gave birth to twin gorillas and the guy who turned into a Fig Newton," I said sarcastically.

"I understand the competition is stiff today, Doc, but there's a lot more I need to tell you about my dream," he added.

Giving Wes's dream its proper attention, I said, "Go ahead and start at the beginning."

"Well, in my dream I woke up in the morning, and I sort of rolled out of bed. As I stood up, I realized I was wearing my normal work clothes—that is, I was wearing a jacket, but I was not wearing any pants. That alone ought to move me past the Fig Newton guy," he mused.

"Very humorous, Wes, but radio rule number one—never be funnier than the host. Please continue," I prompted.

"Anyway, even though I was only wearing underwear with my suit jacket, shirt, and tie, shoes and socks, for some reason I didn't even try to find my pants. I went downstairs to have a cup of coffee, and I was about to head out the door to work when in walked a big red goose. It laid this golden egg in front of me. I picked up the egg and cracked it open, and inside was a bunch of magic fruit seeds. Actually I don't know how I knew they were magic. I just knew. Are you following this, Doc?" Wes asked.

"Big red goose, golden egg, magic fruit seeds. You're moving up the list, Wes. Proceed," I said while scribbling notes.

"So I went into my backyard with this golden egg full of fruit tree seeds, and there was a big area of fresh cow manure that looked like it had been prepared for planting. I took a handful of seeds and started spreading them out in the manure. As soon as the seeds hit the poop . . . can I say *poop* on the air?" he asked.

"You just did, so carry on," I replied.

"Anyhow, as soon as they hit the you know what, they started to grow. I mean *bang!* It looked like one of those time-lapse commercials where everything grows extra fast. Anyway, this one seedling took off and started to grow so fast that I got scared and ran back into my house. I could see through each window in my house that the seed was growing into a tree, which was now so huge it blocked out the sun. I raced to the door, but the tree had sealed all the doors and windows shut and made it pitch-black inside. I ran to the phone to call for help, but as soon as I picked up the receiver, I could hear the noise of the tree growing on the other end. It made sort of a creaking and cracking sound as it grew out of control until it encircled my house. I was trapped inside my home, and I knew I was going to die. That's when I woke up," Wes concluded.

"Pretty psychotic dream, Wes," I chided him. "Great dream symbols and a very clear theme emerged about halfway through that I think hold the key to its meaning. Before I tell you what I think your dream means, I want to clarify that your dream makes you sound like you are a religious man. Is that correct?" I asked.

"I'm a deeply committed Christian," he replied.

"Have you been praying about some event or decision lately?" I asked.

"Yes," Wes replied.

"This may be hard to recall, but do you remember if you prayed about this event or decision prior to going to sleep the night you last had this dream?" I questioned.

"Actually that's not hard at all," Wes stated. "It was two nights ago. My wife and I were in a Bible study, and during the prayer time, I requested the group pray for me in one specific area of my life."

"You told me that in your dream you were wearing most of your work clothes, that is, your suit jacket, shirt, and tie, but no pants. Therefore, your emerging dream theme points toward work or employment. So for now it appears you've been considering and praying about a job change that you're not sure about," I explained.

"Okay, I know I didn't tell your screener anything about that," he said incredulously. "But what about the fruit trees and that goose?"

"I'll walk you through it, Wes," I assured him, "but when we're finished, please give me your opinion of whether this seems to be a self-initiated or God-initiated dream."

"You got it," Wes replied.

"In act one of your dream you've set the theme for the rest of the play. As I said earlier, by virtue of the first few symbols having something to do with starting your day, such as rolling out of bed and the fact you're in your work clothes, we know that your dream play is work related. That much we've established.

"Then you throw in a little twist by mentioning that you aren't wearing any pants, but you don't even try to find them. Not wearing pants denotes insecurity and anxiety over some aspect of your life. Generally it points to a fear that you feel unprepared to accomplish something important. It can also mean you secretly don't think you can handle a situation and you fear you'll be revealed or exposed as inadequate or even an impostor.

"And for my listeners whose minds may be in the gutter, not wearing your pants to work has nothing whatsoever to do with sex. In fact, it's one of the few dream symbols that means essentially the same thing for kids as it does for adults. At some time in their lives, most kids dream they are on their way to school minus their pants. No shot at schools, but it's probably the only subtraction they did the entire school day. Whereas Freud might have had a repressed Oedipal field day with this, it really means the child feels ill prepared for a quiz or test, or he didn't do his homework or study. As for the specifics of your anxiety, Wes, it's safe to assume that since we're focused on work, you're feeling anxious, unprepared, or afraid you'll be exposed as inadequate over some work-based decision. Are you hanging in there with me?" I asked.

"I'm taking notes," Wes replied.

"As act two begins, your dream continues to point toward work in that you are downstairs having a cup of coffee and about to head out the door. Now your subconscious tosses in a rather intriguing and unusual symbol. A big red goose walks in your door and lays a golden egg in front of you. This symbol is difficult to decipher in that geese can mean different things. Generally a honking goose is believed to represent an annoyance while flying geese point to a subconscious desire to get away from routine or something uncomfortable. But a *red* goose that walks into your kitchen—that's a different matter altogether, Wes.

"I think, however, you may have provided me with the tip-off in your next dream symbol. This is where our goose friend lays a golden egg. What do you think of when I say these three words: *goose, gold,* and *egg?*" I asked.

"I think of the fairy-tale story of the goose that lays golden eggs," Wes answered.

"Precisely!" I said encouragingly. "And I'm tempted to go there with you in your work-related dream. It's an easy connection that you've been praying about a job that you hope will produce riches and that job got dropped in your lap. That may be it, but it's important not to lock in on the first connection that seems to make sense because it could be wrong. Then that wrong interpretation pollutes subsequent interpretations. I suggest we depart from the fairy-tale connotation because of the goose's color and because the egg isn't solid gold. Instead, it contains magic fruit seeds."

"Yeah, what's up with the magic fruit seeds?" Wes interjected.

"It's what you did with the seeds that points us to what this may all be about," I replied. "You took them into your backyard where you found a big patch of cow ... how about we say *manure* ... that had been prepared for planting. The symbols here are a backyard and fresh cow manure, which, by the way, is the first time I've encountered cow manure in a dream. Congratulations, Wes."

"Deeply honored," he acknowleged.

"You've heard me talk about the symbol home being a metaphor for oneself. Therefore, backyard in dreams usually denotes something close to home as in the phrase 'right in my own backyard.' The cow manure strikes me as a metaphor for fertile soil. Work with me here, Wes. You're a religious guy, so what do you think of when I mention fertile soil and fruit seeds?"

"I think of Jesus and the parable that good trees produce good fruit and bad trees produce bad fruit," Wes responded.

"Excellent job, Wes. I think that passage in Matthew [Matt. 7:17] speaks to your dream, but I think there may be a more pertinent passage at work here. Do you recall the parable Jesus taught in Luke [Luke 13:6–8] regarding the fig tree in the vineyard that did not produce fruit?" I asked.

"Vaguely," Wes said. "Wasn't that the one about the vineyard boss telling his worker to cut the tree down if it didn't produce fruit?"

"Exactly," I confirmed. "And the key was that the worker asked a favor of his boss, which was . . ."

"He asked for some time to tend to the tree and to fertilize around it to see if it would bear fruit," Wes interrupted.

"Now I think you're on the right track, Wes, and I believe act three of your dream will prove us right," I encouraged him.

"Act three stars you spreading a handful of seeds out in the fertile soil. Instantly one fruit tree takes off and grows so fast that you become frightened and run back into your house. Remember—we're still focusing on work from your earlier symbols, so these new symbols tell us that something work related has taken off so fast that you're afraid of what might happen. In your dream, your fear drove you back into your house, toward safety. Again, since *house* is a metaphor for *you*, that means you see some work-related issue taking off so quickly that it frightens you and makes you feel like retreating to the comfort of what is safe and familiar."

"Okay, Doc," Wes said. "Everything's starting to make sense to me now . . . that is, except for that freaky red goose."

Collecting my thoughts for a moment, I said, "The goose has some special significance that is unique to you. The odd thing is, a red goose has a special significance to me too. When I was a kid, there was a shoe company called Red Goose. I don't know if they're around anymore, but my parents used to make me wear these black corrective wing tip shoes that were very uncomfortable. I'm not sure how old you are, Wes, but is it possible that Red Goose shoes are stuck in your memory somewhere?"

"Oh, my gosh," Wes said excitedly. "I actually do remember Red Goose shoes. I had a few pairs growing up, and now that you mention it, they came with a gold plastic egg that was a piggy bank. There was a toy inside too."

"I know you've probably got this thing pieced together, but don't tell the audience or me what it is yet. Now the task is to connect the theme of shoes or childhood or bank to something that is work related in your life today. Something that you may feel unqualified or overwhelmed about starting. The magic seeds that you planted tell us that it may be a job that sprang up out of nowhere that dominates your current thoughts," I said.

Concluding, I said, "In the final act of your dream drama, you reveal how the fruit tree has consumed your home and trapped you. This represents how your potential job appears all-consuming. Then because the tree cuts off all exits and sunlight, you're revealing how you fear being trapped and perhaps cut off from friends and family if you take this job," I stated.

"Now I need to ask you about your profession. What do you do, Wes?" I asked.

"I'm CEO of US Shopper Dot Com," he said. "We're an Internet home shopping service."

"Okay, then I was wrong in the direction I was thinking," I announced. "I thought because of the connection between the red goose and shoes that you might be in the shoe or apparel industry."

"I'm not, but I have been offered a job by one of the largest shoe manufacturers in the U.S. to move to the East Coast and start up its new Internet initiative," Wes revealed. "Now it makes sense. I do see this job as a great opportunity, but it's a bit overwhelming and I've been praying that God would help me to decide if I really want to uproot my family and move. And to be honest, I've been praying and asking God to look down the road for me to see whether my wife and I would be happy, secure, and satisfied if we go."

"I'm a bit biased, Wes, because if you move, I lose a listener," I added.

"Don't let that influence your opinion because I usually listen to sports on the radio, but there are no games today," Wes joked.

"Then by all means, you're free to move," I joked back. "But getting back to business, Wes, keep in mind that relatively few dreams are divinely inspired. This dream could simply be your mind's way of venting excess anxiety. In essence, these are things you already know and are praying about for guidance."

"All kidding aside, Doc, and I do understand what you're saying, but my family, friends, and I have been praying for clarity and God's leading on this issue. If I'm open to His direction all day, I guess I should be open to His direction at night too. Maybe I'm wrong, but I've got to think He finally got through to me, and I don't have peace about taking this job," Wes declared confidently.

EPILOGUE

Wes's dream presented a compelling case that God indeed chooses to speak to us through dreams. The scientist part of my brain tried to start out with the assumption that the dream was *not* divinely inspired. I placed the burden of proof on the dream and the dreamer's spirituality to convince me otherwise. In this scenario, we had a spiritual man who had submitted options to God and asked for clarity and direction through prayer.

Further evidence that his dream could be divinely inspired was bolstered by the fact that Wes's family, friends, and prayer partners from church had joined him in praying for God's direction in this decision.

The issue for me, then, became not one of *whether* God spoke to Wes through his dream, but *why* God chose the dream over other methods He has at His disposal. Was it that Wes didn't hear or recognize God's leading in other ways, or was it that God chose to open the lines of communication through a dream? I hope one day I'll have an opportunity to ask Him, but for now, I have concluded that God chose to speak to Wes through a dream—simply because He can.

CASE NOTES:

The Ball of Fire Nightmare

NAME: Ron
AGE: 44
OCCUPATION: Pharmaceutical salesman
MARITAL STATUS: Married 18 years, with 3 children
(ages 16, 13, and 10)

Knowing that I have an interest in dreams and that I was pulling together research for this book, a pastor friend called me to ask if I would like to speak to a church member he knew. The pastor told me that one of his congregation members, Ron, had experienced what he thought was a miraculous and clear example of how God could speak to a believer through dreams.

We met at a fast-food restaurant because Ron lived a considerable distance from my office. A devoted husband and father, Ron came across as a deeply spiritual man. He regularly attends my pastor friend's Baptist church and serves on their board of directors. In short, Ron is a credible witness.

Whenever I interview those who believe they have encountered divine dreams, it's beneficial to first gain an understanding of their spiritual lives and their basic knowledge of dreams. Raised in a strong Baptist family, Ron prayed to receive Christ at the age of seventeen at youth camp. He devotes about fifteen minutes a morning to prayer and devotion time, and as for dreams, Ron stated he has read the scriptural accounts of dreams and how God used dreams to communicate with several people in the Bible.

"I've never encountered anything like this dream before," he said as he returned to our table with a fresh cup of coffee. "I would just like your opinion one way or the other. If it's just a weird set of circumstances and not from God, I'm fine with that."

I acknowledged his request and asked him to tell me his dream.

"I was away on business, which I hate because I'm the worrying type. I worry that someone might break into the house, that one of the kids will get hurt, that the dog will get out. You name it and it's on my daily worry-and-pray list when I'm away. My wife will tell you—I'm a worrywart," he said, smiling.

I assured him that I, too, was a member of the worrywart club. We shared a laugh, and then he continued with his dream.

"Well, the night before I was due to come home from my sales trip I had this disturbing, nonsensical nightmare," Ron said. "I mean, it scared me to death, even though it wasn't one of those horror movie–type nightmares people have. This one startled me right out of bed, but it wasn't because it seemed so real.

"It's odd, too, because there just wasn't much to the dream unless I'm blocking out a lot of it. It was probably over in a minute. I dreamed that the sun had somehow dropped from the sky and was suspended by two pieces of wire, one black and one white, directly over my home. As it lowered, I could make out the image of a thermostat implanted in its side. It's just like the thermostat that controls the heating and air-conditioning in my home. It's one of those with a clock in it, and you can set it to come on and go off at certain times. Then the sun continued to drop until it stopped ten feet from my roof."

I asked him where he was when he observed this, and he explained that he was standing in front of his house like a spectator, just staring at the thermostat. Ron could see the date on the thermostat's readout was June 12, which was the actual date of his dream. He could also see the time, but instead of its reading the normal hours and minutes, it was counting down from fifteen minutes toward zero.

"I can see it just as clearly now as I saw it in my dream. The sun was blazing hot, and I could feel the heat coming from it and see the lavalike eruptions on its surface. Then still suspended by the two wires, the sun started moving slowly all around my house, like it was searching for a place to touch down. Finally it stopped over my garage.

"From where I was standing I could see that the timer on the thermostat had hit ten minutes just as it melted through the two suspending wires, which sent it crashing through my roof. Then I saw it had started a fire in my garage, and I heard my dog barking and running around the house, trying to wake someone up. I knew I couldn't do anything to help. I just stood on the sidewalk as the fire spread through my home and consumed my family."

"Fascinating dream, Ron," I said calmly. "Do you recall the feeling you had when you awakened from it?"

"Yes, but that's strange too," he replied. "I was scared, but I was very calm. That seemed weird to me that I'd just had a dream where my family died in a house fire, and as disturbing as that image was, I had a calm resolve about it."

"When you say 'resolve,'" I inquired, "what do you mean?"

"I mean the only way I can describe it is that it was as if I were using an emergency response that had been tested over and over until it became routine. It was as if I were the only calm one. I also got this sense that the timer was still counting down, and I had to do something before it reached zero."

He explained that he had an overwhelming sense that his next step was to contact his wife. "I knew that if I didn't, my family would die in a fire," Ron said without a trace of doubt.

"Okay, Ron. So at this point you're fully awake from your dream. You have what you call a calm resolve, but also an overwhelming sense that you need to call home to reach your wife. What did you do next?" I probed.

"I called home and woke my wife from a dead sleep," he said. "I didn't tell her that I'd had a dream. I just said I had a real uneasy feeling that something was wrong, and then I asked her to check through the house just to set my mind at ease."

"And she did as you asked?" I inquired.

"Yeah. She came back after about two minutes and said everything was just fine. She called me a worrywart and asked if she could go back to sleep. That's when it hit me that the fire in my nightmare didn't take place in the house; it took place in the garage," he added.

"I asked her to humor me and to please, please check the garage. She said I was nuts, and I'm not sure she wasn't about to hang up on me when she heard our dog barking at something, so she got up to check and left me there on the phone. Then about five minutes later, she came back to the phone all out of breath and said one thing: 'How did you know? How did you know?'

She repeated that about a dozen times until I finally told her it came to me in a dream."

"And what did she tell you once everything calmed down?" I asked.

"My wife told me that she smelled smoke coming from the garage, and when she opened the door, she saw that our furnace had caught fire and the insulation around the ventilator ducts was burning quickly. She grabbed a fire extinguisher that I keep in the garage and was able to put the fire out," Ron stated. "But the really freaky part came when I got home the following morning and inspected the damage.

"I had a buddy of mine from the fire department stop by to take a look at the furnace with me. He said that it looked like an electrical short and then pointed to these two wires at the top of the furnace. He showed me how the old insulation around the white wire had melted away, which allowed it to touch the black wire, causing a short. Because I have an old home without a circuit breaker attached to the furnace, the short sent sparks around the furnace area, which eventually caught on fire. He said these fires are rare, but when they do occur, they can be devastating because the smoke shoots through the vents and into the rooms so everyone ends up in a world of hurt from smoke inhalation," Ron concluded.

Ron and I discussed his dream over the next half hour or so. As dreams go, Ron was correct that his was brief. It also provided relatively few symbols with which to work. I didn't tell Ron yet that this was often the case with dreams that seem to have a divine origin.

I said, "Ron, the first symbol you provide is that of being a bystander or observer in your dream. This simply connects to your being away from home and to your sense of helplessness while away. That much is easy.

"Your next symbols, the black and white wires, are also easy. The wires represent electricity, which provides the power to your third symbol—the sun. In your dream, the sun denotes a fiery, potentially fatal object," I said, pausing to think. "It's the thermostat that intrigues me most because it carries several connotations. It's implanted in the sun, which could represent a ticking time bomb. Or because it is the same thermostat that governs the furnace and air-conditioning in your home, it could just be an abstract connection in your mind to the heat of the sun and your home.

"Ultimately, though, I'd come down on the side that it represents the ticking time bomb because it was counting down from fifteen minutes. Since thermostat clocks don't do this normally, we have to assume this plays a major role in your dream . . . one that denotes a sense of urgency to accomplish something before the clock reaches zero."

"What about hearing my dog barking and running around the house?" Ron asked.

"Probably attributable to a logical connection to what was going on in your dream. That much is similar to dreams about a car accident that might often be accompanied by sirens," I offered.

"Then what's your verdict?" he inquired.

"Ron, there are only four possibilities to consider. Actually three, after I discounted the possibility that you may be mentally unstable early on. No offense," I said.

Ron nodded and assured me that he, too, would want to establish that if he were investigating dreams.

"The three remaining possibilities are, number one, God, or an agent of God, truly visited you in your dream; number two, you had a premonition in your sleep; or number three, the entire scenario was nothing more than an amazing coincidence.

"Just so you understand how I work through these scenarios, Ron, the scientist part of me has to look at the nonreligious-related possibilities first because they are far more common than divinely inspired dreams. I want to think about your dream for twenty-four hours, and I'll call you and let you know what I think," I explained.

Ron agreed, and we ended our meeting.

Epilogue

Examining the possibility that Ron's dream could be chalked up to a great coincidence, I asked a mathematician colleague to run some numbers for me. He calculated that the odds for (a) Ron to awaken from his sleep while away from home, (b) from a specific dream about fire, (c) with specific dream symbols that pinpoint the origin of the fire, (d) at the specific time that a fire was breaking out in his home, and then (e) to convince his wife to check the house are roughly 952 million to one. He added that it would be statistically more likely that Ron would have won his state's lottery thirty-six days in a row—without ever buying a ticket!

Discounting the great coincidence theory, the next argument might be that Ron had a premonition in his sleep. Although this theory is statistically more plausible than the preceding, one cannot discount the fact that premonitions are a controversial and yet unproven belief. Many scientists, myself included, believe that what some call premonitions are actually dreams that occur in light, near awake stages of sleep or in mild trancelike states. Most of us can relate to times when we are awake, perhaps even doing something, and we lose a moment where our brains sort of "checked out."

While there is such a thing as intuition and sensitivity to the likelihood of future events, science has struggled to prove the existence of premonitions. Yet scientifically minded people have recognized and studied dreams since the beginning of time. Still, to be fair, these same scientists will tell you that God-ordained dreams are far less scientifically provable. At some point, faith and logic converge to point to a more plausible theory.

An undeniable factor that raises a strong argument that Ron's dream was divinely inspired is that he is a deeply religious man. If Ron is tuned into God on multiple levels while awake, doesn't it make sense that he would be more likely to be receptive to Him while asleep?

Finally, even if we were to stipulate that premonitions do indeed exist, how do we reconcile the belief that they are experienced only while awake, and Ron clearly stated he was sleeping when he had his? While it is impossible to calculate the odds in this scenario, a scientist would have to concede that this is a highly improbable theory as well.

That left me with the much more mathematically plausible theory that Ron's dream was divinely inspired. As you've seen already, divine intervention begs the second question: Why? Why does God intervene in some cases and not others? Or is it possible He intervenes frequently but only in the dreams of people with a spiritual sensitivity who acknowledge and seek His presence? Again, these are questions I pray I'll have a chance to ask one day.

To the scientist who believes in God, Ron's dream is consistent with how God delivered warning dreams throughout the Bible. This individual has a much easier time with a divine explanation than he does with the mathematical improbability of all the circumstances happening by chance.

However, to the nonbelieving scientist, it is much more plausible to believe that the whole scenario was a fantastic coincidence or that Ron set the whole thing up to collect on insurance money. Either way, it would take a lot more faith to come to these conclusions than to accept that God was warning Ron of the fire. Sounds reasonable to me.

I called Ron and shared my theory with him the following day. We both concurred and prayed together, thanking God for His mercy.

CASE NOTES:

The Thirty-Nine-Year Nightmare

NAME: Elizabeth
AGE: 52
OCCUPATION: Homemaker
MARITAL STATUS: Married 28 years, with 2 children
(ages 26 and 19)

E lizabeth telephoned my office to make an appointment concerning what she termed a "very disturbing dream" that she had been having since she was thirteen years old. I was eager to meet with her because it is extremely rare to interview subjects with a recurring dream spanning thirty-nine years.

As first impressions go, Elizabeth struck me as a successful business-person. She arrived five minutes early dressed in a navy blue pinstriped business suit and carrying a briefcase. She appeared as though she would be going straight from her session to a Fortune 500 board meeting.

Addressing me as Doctor Cynaumon and bearing no trace of a smile, Elizabeth sat down, opened her briefcase, and took out a check register, stating that she wanted to pay before the session began.

I calmly explained that I didn't want to take her money until I had an opportunity to help her. From experience, I knew that controlling types often use money as a way of trying to gain the upper hand in therapy.

She appeared perplexed and commented on how she had just assumed I was like the other psychologists she had seen, who had wanted her money up front.

Curious, I asked how many therapists she had seen.

43

She explained that she had lost count, and that after her father died, she had first seen someone when she was thirteen. She claimed he was a quack and perhaps something of a pervert too.

My confused look gave me away, so she explained that she had gone to see the man once a week for more than two years. Usually he would ask her how her week had gone, she would say fine, and then he would stare at her for the rest of the session, which lasted another forty-five minutes. She then explained the assumption that he was a pervert, stating that he asked her inappropriate questions regarding whether she had had sexual dreams and so forth and then stared at her in a way that made Elizabeth very uncomfortable.

I promised not to ask about boyfriends and said I would face the wall if that would help her.

She smiled for the first time and appeared to relax.

I asked further questions about her dream and any other professionals she had consulted in order to understand it.

"I've probably told five or six doctors about my dream," she said cavalierly as she settled into her chair. "I've even told it to a tarot card reader, two fortune-tellers, a priest, and a gypsy woman who told me I'd be hit by a train on my fortieth birthday."

I tried not to smile and asked her to relay what she had learned from the remaining experts.

Taking a deep breath, she said, "I learned that tarot card readers think fortune-tellers are shysters. Gypsies don't trust anyone who is not Greek, and priests think the whole lot of them are an exorcism looking for a place to happen.

"In all seriousness, Doctor, I have told many so-called professionals about my recurring nightmare. It's frustrating because they all had an opinion of what my dream meant, but none of them agreed. It seemed so pointless after a while that I gave up. The dream even went away for about a year, but then it started up again," she concluded.

I nodded and asked her to continue.

"Like I said, I was thirteen years old when I started having this dream. In my dream, my father was going away on a business trip, and we were all going to see him off at the train station. For some reason, he left before we did and arrived at the train station ahead of us. As we arrived, we walked down to the train platform, and I saw that the train was already starting to move. This was upsetting to me because I wanted to say good-bye. Then I saw my dad. He was seated, looking out the window at me, and I could see tears in his eyes," she said with an emotionless voice that came from repeating the story again and again.

"Then he stood up, and I could see that my dad was holding a beautifully wrapped gift. It was wrapped with very expensive paper and had a bright pink ribbon on top. As soon as he saw me, he held the present out the window, and I started running alongside the moving train. As the train picked up speed, he leaned farther and farther out until his upper body was outside the train window. The train kept picking up speed as I frantically tried to reach my father to receive my gift. At one point, I was within a half inch of touching the present. Then he smiled at me, but it wasn't his normal smile. It was sort of a desperate, forced smile, as if he knew it was hopeless and we couldn't reach each other."

Staring blankly at the floor, Elizabeth finished her story, explaining that she gave up, even though she was sure that she could have run faster and caught up with him. She returned to the train station to where her mother and brothers were waiting. They were all crying and dressed in black.

Elizabeth's eyes were full of tears as she explained that she just wanted to know what it all meant and what her dad's gift was to her. She explained that if she could, perhaps the nightmare would be put to rest.

Hers was a particularly difficult dream to interpret, but not so much because of the dream's symbolism and themes. Actually those were quite vivid and meaningful. The difficult part of her dream was that she had lived with it for so many years and repeated it to so many others that Elizabeth had become cynical and jaded about the varied interpretations. I also knew that there was a good chance that parts of my interpretation might be similar to some she'd heard. I asked her to tell me if there was anything about the dream that she already understood.

"Well, Doctor, the most that I've been able to understand over the years has been that since my dad was on a train and leaving for a long trip, he must have been dead. Everyone has been able to tell me that. Some say he was going to heaven, and others have said he was just leaving the family on a journey," she said, pausing. "But nobody can tell me what's inside the package, and I've got to know or I think I will eventually go crazy."

I agreed with her completely that the dream signified the father was embarking on a journey. I felt it was time to move on to some of the more in-depth pieces of the dream. I asked when her father had passed away.

She admitted it had happened when she was thirteen. He had died of a heart attack while he was away on business. She went on to explain about their relationship without my having to ask, smiling as she relayed that he had called her his "fairy princess." She was the only girl in the family and had several brothers. She wanted to know if perhaps her father was trying to communicate with her through the dream, wherever he might be.

I explained that I wasn't a psychic, and that though it might be wonderful to think he was sending a message to her through this dream, there is no evidence that we are able to communicate with departed loved ones. I explained further that though I know God is in charge of all things, and that He could allow this to happen, there is no evidence to support this conclusion.

She nodded understandingly and asked me to continue to interpret the dream for her anyway.

"Elizabeth, I need you to go back in your mind to your early teen years. Close your eyes and remember the home you lived in. Remember your dad and how much you loved him and what he meant to you. Are you with me?" I asked.

"Yes."

"Fine. Now tell me. Did your father go away often on business trips, or did he work close to home?" I inquired.

"He worked close to home, but about once a year, he would go to a big convention in another city. He would take the train and be gone for a few days."

"I understand. When he came home, would he bring you a gift?"

Smiling, she replied, "Yes. He would always bring home something small for each of us kids. But he never brought home anything as large and extravagantly wrapped as the gift he's trying to give me in my dreams."

"That's helpful," I said. "What month did your father pass away, Elizabeth?"

"I distinctly recall it being in August because we were all out of school," she answered.

"And your birthday is in what month?" I inquired, trying not to let her get too far in front of me in the interpretation.

"My birthday . . ." She paused. "My birthday is September first."

"Elizabeth, is it possible you are feeling guilty about something you said or did prior to your father's leaving on that business trip in August?"

Her voice increased in both volume and pitch as she replied, "What do you mean 'guilty'? Why would you ask me such a terrible thing?"

Calmly I explained that I wasn't trying to hurt her and that she had come to me in search of the meaning of this dream. I made it clear that it was up to her whether we continued with the session or stopped right where we were. She nodded quickly and assured me she did want to continue.

"Good, Elizabeth. Now think back to the time just prior to your thirteenth birthday. Tell me about your relationship with your parents back then."

Elizabeth sat silently staring at the wall for what I would estimate to be five minutes. Then tears began to well up in her eyes, and she reached into her purse for a tissue.

"Do you want to tell me about it?" I inquired.

"Yes," she said. "My dad and I were really distant at that time. We almost never fought, but he was really disappointed in me just before my thirteenth birthday."

I nodded understandingly and asked her to continue, assuring her that she was doing very well.

"I had a boyfriend, a guy about three years older than myself, and my dad didn't like him very much. He and my mom used to tell me that a guy that old was only after one thing in a young teenager. They were really against him because he had dropped out of high school and was working at a gas station down the street from our home."

"Something significant happened between your father and you then, didn't it?" I asked, although I already knew the answer.

"My dad was only trying to help. I know he loved me, and he was just looking out for me," she asserted defensively.

"Elizabeth," I said, "there's no doubt in my mind that your father loved you, and everything he did was done out of love. But you need to tell me what happened."

"He went over to my boyfriend's work and told him that he didn't want him to see me anymore. He didn't threaten him or anything like that. He just told him that I was too young for him. And then my boyfriend broke up with me."

"And what happened between you and your father after that?"

With my question, Elizabeth broke down and sobbed for several minutes before gaining enough composure to answer, "I told him that I hated him and that I would never forgive him for coming between my boyfriend and me."

"Elizabeth, can you recall how long it was after that event that your father left town on his business trip?"

"I've never thought about it," she said as she searched around the walls and ceiling as if the answer was posted somewhere. "I guess . . . now that I think about it, it was about a week or two after my boyfriend and I broke up," she concluded. "Yes, it was because I remember that we split up right before my birthday."

"And if we're putting the pieces of the time puzzle together, I'm recollecting that you told me that your father passed away just prior to your birthday on September first. Was that right?" I asked so that Elizabeth could see the pieces coming together.

She asserted that he had passed away within a week of her thirteenth birthday.

It was time for Elizabeth to begin to understand why she had endured this recurring nightmare for thirty-nine years. I started by explaining that her dream had been set in motion by the second strongest human emotion, guilt (the first being love), and that she had been living with monumental levels of repressed guilt over the fight between her and her father as well as the words she had said to him. I asked her if she wanted to continue.

She assured me she didn't want to turn back after getting this far.

I wanted to help her put this nightmare to rest, so I said, "It's apparent that you've been dealing with unresolved guilt. The guilt couldn't have been resolved by virtue of the fact that, until today, you hadn't remembered even having that argument with your dad. You've been suffering through these dreams because your subconscious mind has been trying to make you look at the guilt you've felt through the years. The nightmare returns over and over in an attempt to get you to deal with the reality that you feel tremendous guilt about saying harsh things to someone you loved very much just prior to his passing away. Tell me, Elizabeth, did you love him?"

With her head down, Elizabeth stared at the floor. Teardrops collected on the purse she held on her lap. "That's the worst part, Doctor. I was closer to my dad than anyone in the world," she answered.

"There seems to be no doubt how your father felt about you. Didn't you tell me you were his 'fairy princess'—growing up in a house full of frogs for brothers?" I said, trying to lighten the mood. "So, as they say in court, let's stipulate to the fact that you and your father had a very special relationship. Is that safe to say?"

She nodded affirmatively and smiled through her tears.

"Then let's look at this another way, shall we?" I asked.

Nodding, Elizabeth looked straight into my eyes and prepared herself.

"Do you have children?" I inquired.

"Two," she replied, smiling.

"Has one of them ever told you he hates you?"

"Of course," she said, "that's just part of being a . . ."

"That's just part of being a kid. Isn't that what you were going to say?"

"Yes," she confirmed. "That is just part of being a kid."

"I've got two kids, Elizabeth. And I seem to recall a time or two when they said they hated their mom or me for some reason or another. I couldn't tell you when or why, and I'm sure they couldn't, either. The reason none of us could tell you when or why they'd say something momentarily hurtful is that there was no mile marker stuck next to it. What you said to your dad was no better or worse than what any other teenager says in anger to a parent. Had some time elapsed between those words and your father's passing, you likely would have no recollection of the incident. But the fact is, time did not pass, and you've been stuck, standing next to that mile marker for thirty-nine years. Thirty-nine years of trying to block out the guilt and thirty-nine years of your subconscious trying to force you to deal with it."

I encouraged her to face the truth that our kids say things and don't mean them, just as we ourselves said things to our own parents and didn't mean them. It was crucial for her to understand this to get over the guilt that was repressing her.

With a look of relief Elizabeth nodded her head and said she did understand.

"Now let's crack the code and reveal once and for all what was inside the package your father was trying to hand you from the train, okay?" I said.

"Okay, let's go for it," she agreed nervously.

"Let's begin by understanding that you described the gift as a beautiful large package with a pink bow on top. That tells me there could be no mistake about the intended recipient of the gift. You knew it was intended just for you—his fairy princess. Does that make sense so far?" I asked.

"There is no doubt in my mind the gift was for me," she answered.

"Elizabeth, receiving a gift in a dream usually denotes the dreamer anticipated receiving something fortunate or life changing. The gift you created in your dream was unusually large and extraordinarily beautiful. Therefore, we know that whatever your mind created inside the box was going to be extremely fortunate and life changing for you," I continued.

"Now let's look at the next dream symbol, which you described as *straining* to reach each other. Straining in dreams denotes something difficult, but with a positive outcome and generally worth the effort. Because your father was straining to *give* the gift to you, we know that the life-changing content of your gift was something that had to come from him. We also know it would be difficult to get it to you, but once you had it, it would be worth the effort. That, in a nutshell, is how you viewed the gift and his attempt to pass it to you," I said, pausing to allow Elizabeth to gather it all in.

Elizabeth's eyes widened as she said, "I get it! I really understand what you're saying. Don't stop! Tell me what was in the box. What was my dad's gift to me?"

"You know what was in the box, Elizabeth," I said calmly. "You don't need me to tell you what his gift to you was. Just close your eyes, and imagine the most precious gift he could have given you. A gift that would have made these past thirty-nine years easier in relation to his memory. Elizabeth, what was in the box?" I asked.

"Forgiveness," she said as she broke down, sobbing. "He was handing me the gift of forgiveness and his love. His gift was that we were okay! He knew I didn't mean what I'd said."

I waited for Elizabeth to look up at me before saying, "You are correct, and you now understand your dream."

EPILOGUE

As a clinical aside, Elizabeth's case was the longest-running recurring nightmare I've personally encountered. I recalled there being a handful of cases documented in psychiatric journals where dreams spanned forty to fifty years, but they are extremely rare.

Several dream symbols appeared in Elizabeth's recurring dream. It's very important not to get distracted by multiple dream symbols and miss the dream's true meaning. This could have been the case with Elizabeth's dream. Clearly the key to unlocking her dream and freeing her from her guilt prison was predominantly the passing of the gift between her father and her as well as the gift itself. However, there were other symbols of interest.

Trains, for instance, symbolize much of what you'd expect them to mean. Although Freud attached a sexual connotation to trains, which we will skip here, I've found them to denote a journey. More precisely trains tend to represent longer and slower journeys through life while airplanes often represent freedom or release.

Another prominent symbol was that Elizabeth's father was standing half inside and half outside at the window of the train. She created this symbol to represent her belief that her father half wanted to go on his previously mentioned life journey and half wanted to stay with her. Pressing further into this symbol and in a later conversation, she told me that her father was a deeply religious man. She confirmed that he had a strong relationship with God and believed heaven was a wonderful place. Therefore, in her dream, she created a scenario where her father was at peace with leaving for his trip to heaven but wanted her to receive his gift of forgiveness first.

Elizabeth provided another helpful symbol when she gave up trying to reach her father and returned to the station where her mother and brothers were seated. She stated they wore dark clothing, which denotes that her family was already grieving the loss and moving on, while she was stuck in disbelief, which was driven by her guilt and grief.

Two weeks passed before I heard from Elizabeth. She called to say that she had not had her recurring dream since her session, but that the previous night had featured an unusual twist to her usual dream. She dreamed about her father leaning out the window of the train to give her the gift, but this time, she received it. She told me that she carried the gift back to the same bench where previously her mother and brothers were seated. This time it was only Elizabeth sitting on the bench. Carefully she untied the beautiful pink bow and folded back the expensive pink paper. Removing the lid, she found the box was full to overflowing with those little Styrofoam packing peanuts. She said she knew that there was nothing else inside the box, but she laughed and had a great time running her hands through the packing peanuts.

As unusual as packing peanuts are in a dream, I accepted Elizabeth's interpretation of their meaning. She believed that each Styrofoam piece represented good feelings like love, happiness, and forgiveness and, above all, great memories of her father. She said that's why it made her so happy in her dream to just sit and run her fingers through them.

Although Elizabeth's quest to understand her dream had lasted far too long, it did provide a beautiful message of healing. To the question of whether or not it was inspired from God, I would answer *no*, followed by *yes*. Specifically I believe the origin of her recurring dream was created by guilt inside her subconscious. Like an irritating grain of sand in an oyster, it could eventually produce something beautiful, or it could remain a useless irritation for life. I believe God was finally successful in getting Elizabeth's attention long enough to provide her with the tools to understand her dream.

CASE NOTES:

The Nightmare Affair

NAME: Tom
AGE: 37
OCCUPATION: Fireman
MARITAL STATUS: Married 9 years, with 3 children

I had been teaching a series of Sunday school classes on the topic of the Bible and dreams when a husband and wife approached me and requested a moment of my time. There were several people waiting to speak to me, and the man asked if we could step away from the group so he could ask me a private question. Telling the others I'd be right back, I obliged, and we moved to a corner of the room. Next, he turned to his wife and politely asked if she minded that he speak with me alone. She nodded her head and walked away to visit with a friend.

In a hushed tone the man told me that never having been one to dream or pay attention to his dreams, he had been having several *uncomfortable* dreams over the past few months. When asked if he would like to tell me his dream, he opted not to. Instead, he asked if he could schedule an appointment to see me. We scheduled an appointment for the following Wednesday afternoon.

On the morning of his appointment, my answering service relayed a message from Tom that he was canceling his appointment because his dreams had stopped. I laughed and thought how few therapists there must be in the world who can make dreams stop just by making an appointment. I took advantage of the break in my schedule to take care of my favorite activity—completing stacks of insurance billing forms. That and a root canal would just about make a perfect day.

The following morning, Tom called: "Hey, Doc, I'm really sorry for stiffing you on the appointment yesterday. I'd just been feeling so much better after we spoke at church that my nightmares went away, so I thought I was cured."

Having never cured anyone of nightmares before, I considered writing Tom's case up in the psychoanalytic journals or writing a book about it and nominating myself for a Pulitzer Prize. Reining in just a little of my sarcasm, I asked, "But you found out you were reinfected with the dream, did you?"

"That's a good one . . . reinfected," he said. "Yeah, I guess you could say that. Anyhow, Doc, I was wondering if you could see me today. The nightmares are back, and I can't sleep!"

I made an appointment for Tom later that day and waited to see how it would go. Upon his arrival in the office, I told him to make himself at home, and I started by gathering a little information about him and his family.

"I'm a fireman," he stated in typical male fashion, which is to first describe yourself by what you do rather than who you are. "Actually I'm a fire captain. I've got three kids, a nine-year-old from a previous marriage and twin six-year-olds with my current wife. We attend the church you spoke at and . . . what else?" he said as though stumped to find anything else meaningful in his life.

"That's fine," I replied. "Now you told me at church that you were having some recurring nightmares, but then your phone call said they'd stopped."

"Yeah," he said. "I thought I'd rid myself of them, but the night after I canceled my appointment with you, they fired back up again."

"Why don't you tell me a little about the recurring dreams you've been having, but first, what feeling do you awaken with after one of these dreams?" Typical of cops and firemen, the mere mention of the word *feeling* caused his eyes to glaze over slightly and his head to tilt at an angle.

"What do you mean *feeling?*" he quizzed. "You mean what do I feel like during and after my dream? You mean like mad or angry feelings?"

"Those are two feelings among a dozen or so that people commonly feel during and after dreams, Tom," I said. "It's very helpful in understanding the dreams if I can get a sense of how they make you feel."

"Okay, okay . . . I understand what you're asking," he said, gazing up at the ceiling. "I would have to say that I feel scared and impotent."

I was shocked. *Impotent?* Did I hear him right? Did he really say he felt scared and *impotent?* Perhaps I'd underestimated this firefighter's ability to connect with his feelings. *Wait,* I thought. Maybe he meant *important*—scared and *important.* Certainly this merited a closer look. I would figure out which word he meant as we proceeded. "Why don't you tell me about your dreams, Tom?" I asked.

"Well, no time like the present," he said while drawing in a deep breath. "My dreams are all similar. I was working my shift at the FD . . . that means fire department."

"Yes, I actually put that together from my years at the PD, Tom," I replied, smiling.

"Oh, yeah. I forgot you were a cop," he said, returning the smile. "Anyway, the alarm in the station went off, and we started scrambling around to get our gear together and get to the engine to go handle a fire. Everyone was running around and getting prepared, but not me. I was moving in slow motion, and my station commander was hollering at me to get my act together. Then I finally decided it was taking me too long to find all my equipment. I got to the engine and took my seat in front, next to the engineer. We were pulling out of the station and rolling swiftly—code three—to the scene of the fire when I looked down and noticed I wasn't wearing my pants," he said while looking at me out of the corner of his eye to see if I was smiling.

"Please continue," I said, choking back a laugh only to lose it as Tom began laughing.

"This is serious biz, Doc. I was rolling to a fire, and I didn't have my yellow pants on. Forget the embarrassment. Fighting a fire without your pants can be hazardous to your health," he said while laughing. "Besides, my dreams got really scary from that point forward."

Tom continued, "We were en route to the fire when I suddenly realized that the dispatcher had given us my home address. I confirmed the address with her, she repeated it, and sure enough, it was my address.

"Then my station commander ordered me off the engine because he didn't want me fighting a fire at my own home and trying to save my wife and kids. Then he literally pushed me off the engine as it was going about forty miles per hour. As I was rolling and skidding along the pavement, I could see the fire engine continuing down the street to the fire," he said.

"By now, I was panicking that I wouldn't get there in time to save my family from the fire, so I started running toward my home," he said. "But just like back at the fire station, I was running in slow motion. I was carrying a sixty-pound fire hose on my back and running in slow motion toward my house, which was fully engulfed in flames.

"Finally I made it up to my house. Everyone was packing up his gear and walking back to the engine," Tom noted. "I asked my commander what was going on, and he said it was a false alarm. He said that my wife and kids were shaken up, but that there had been no fire. Even though I could see from the outside that my house had been completely destroyed in the blaze, I didn't even check on my family. We all got back onto the engine and headed back to the station, and that's when I woke up."

"Quite a dream," I said admiringly. "Do you want it straight, or would you like me to sugarcoat it for you first?"

"Uh-oh," he replied. "That's never good. Can't it just mean that my work pants don't fit me right and I need to replace them?" he joked.

"I could tell you that, hand you a bill, and send you on your way if that's what you're looking for," I said kindly. "But I get the impression you're not the sugarcoat it kind of guy."

"You're right," he replied, displaying a measure of tenseness for the first time. "Give it to me straight."

"How long have you been having an affair?" I asked while looking straight into his eyes.

Unable to hide the truth, his eyes widened slightly and darted around the room. "What makes you say that?" he asked slowly.

"I'd be happy to reveal the several dream symbols that point to that," I stated. "But it would be beneficial to our progress if you and I were to start out on the same page, so to speak."

"I've been seeing a lady for about four months," Tom said sheepishly.

"Does your wife know?" I asked.

"No," he replied. "But she knows something's wrong in our marriage, and she hoped that if we started going to church together, it would get better. In fact, the Sunday that we heard you speak was only the third time I've been to church in my life."

"Does anyone else know that you're having an affair besides your station commander?" I asked.

"What? . . . oh, my . . . how'd you know that Jack knows?" he said accusingly, as if I'd been opening his mail.

"How else would I know except that your dream revealed it?" I replied.

"You mean when I said he didn't want me to go to a fire at my own house and then pushed me off the engine? That told you that he knew I was having an affair?" Tom inquired.

"That and a few other suggestions did, Tom. It also suggested that your commander is a moral or even religious guy, and not only does he know, but he doesn't approve. Does that ring a bell?" I asked.

"Yeah," Tom said dejectedly. "He's a dyed-in-the-wool, born-again Christian, just like my wife. But why am I having these dreams? In your lecture you said that God is sometimes involved in our dreams, but why would He be on my case? Doesn't He have bigger fish to fry than some firefighter who's having an affair? I mean, I'm not even a Christian. Doesn't God just mess with Christians' heads? I think my dreams are born out of my own coconut and not a God thing. Am I wrong?"

"Not necessarily," I cautioned. "It isn't a stretch at all to believe that God is working on you big time. By that, I mean that He knows you've got one foot planted at home and the other at a girlfriend's place. He knows that you're feeling lost, confused, and more than a little nervous about where your life is heading. Why wouldn't He try to reach you before you make a second huge mistake? And tapping into your dreams is one way He could choose to grab your attention. Maybe He's tried in a number of other areas, but you've been closed off to Him."

"So, if I'm hearing you right, Doc, you think God might be sending me these dreams to get me to move in one direction or the other concerning my wife or my girlfriend?"

"You're half right, Tom," I replied. "I think it very well may be God sending you these dreams, but it isn't to get you to decide *which* woman you intend to stay with."

"How do you know that?" Tom asked sincerely.

"I know that because the Bible tells us that God hates divorce [Mal. 2:16]," I replied. "And one of the surest ways to determine the direction a dream is leading is to check it against the Word of God. God would never want you to do something that He is on record as saying He hates. Check it out for yourself. It's the last book of the Old Testament, right before the Gospel of Matthew, my friend."

"So are you telling me I should tell my wife that I've been having an affair?" Tom asked.

"I understand your anxiety, Tom, but you're getting way out ahead of where we are today. You came to me for dream counseling, not marriage counseling. Therefore, my counsel to you, at least for today, is that you immediately stop the sin and begin to do the right thing. I know you don't know where you stand on the whole Christian issue yet, but the wisest thing you could do for yourself and your family is to sever the relationship immediately with your girlfriend. Only then will you have a ghost of a chance of making wise choices about where you go from here," I said with conviction, but trying not to sound preachy.

"One more note, Tom. If you do decide to take my advice about your affair, I'd like to refer you to a colleague who can help you through it."

Tom stared at me as he nervously tapped his fingers on his knees before saying, "You are right! I went to church the Sunday you were speaking for a reason, and I doubt that was a coincidence. Plus, I'm not the type who wants to talk with someone after a class, so that probably was no coincidence, either. Then I blew off my session with you because I was scared you'd find out about my affair and tell my wife. Then I had the dream again—that couldn't be a coincidence. And you nailed me right between the eyes about my dream. There's too much going on here to say that it's all just a big coincidence. Why don't you go ahead and give me the name of that referral?"

EPILOGUE

A few weeks later I received word from the therapist I'd recommended that Tom and his wife were regularly coming to marriage counseling. Confidentiality and ethical guidelines prevented me from obtaining progress reports.

Many of Tom's dream symbols were relatively easy to discern. On the other hand, some of the symbols offered deeper, more profound meanings and opened the door for divine interpretation. For starters, his dream presented an out-of-control image of scrambling around trying to get his gear together to handle a fire. As a dream symbol, fire can represent several things. Because Tom is a firefighter, fire takes on an expanded meaning. In this case, it represented something dangerous that he is drawn to. When he said that he was moving in slow motion, he was actually saying that he was feeling stuck and somewhat powerless to change the problem.

My first glimpse into his commander being in on the secret of Tom's affair came when he yelled at Tom to get his act together. His commander represented a respected person of authority who was telling Tom that he was out of line. Next, Tom revealed that he was frustrated because it was taking him too much time to find all of his equipment. These symbols described his confusion and overwhelmed feelings over what to do and how long it was taking him to decide.

It doesn't take a conference call between Dr. Freud and Dr. Jung to figure out the next symbol. Tom said he finally got onto the fire engine, and they were on their way to the fire; he looked down and realized he didn't have his pants on. Be cautious not to make the obvious leap that this is a sexual symbol. Not wearing pants in public most often denotes anxiety that something in your life will be revealed, exposed, or discovered. Often these symbols are driven by feelings of guilt, shame, and confusion. In Tom's case, not having pants on revealed his shame and guilt over his affair, coupled with his fear that his wife would discover it.

From there Tom's dream dispatched him to the scene of a fire that happened to be at his home. Again, no postgrad degree is required; you may recall from our previous dream accounts that home is a metaphor for oneself. Therefore, if Tom's home was on fire, this represented the most destructive and deadly threat that Tom's mind could muster.

In the next scene, Tom was running in slow motion toward his burning home. To discern this image, one needs to merely couple the symbols we have already discussed. Slow motion denoted his sense of powerlessness and inability to decide. His burning house was his life going up in flames. By putting the two together, we see his dream has revealed that his anguish is about his inability to decide how to keep from destroying his life.

A wonderful dream symbol and overall image enters next. If it weren't so tragic, it would almost appear as a comedy. Here's a fire captain who forgot his pants and was rolling toward a fire at his home, only to be pushed from the engine by his commander. He started running in slow motion toward the fire, only he was carrying a sixty-pound fire hose on his back. To discern the meaning behind the fire hose, we have to break the symbol into two parts. First up is the hose itself. A hose, in this dream, was simply a delivery system. So what does it deliver? Water. And what does water denote in dreams? Life, healing and, to a fireman in particular, the only way to keep his life from burning up.

In the next scene, he saw his house fully involved (completely on fire), but by the time he made it to his home with the fire hose, the other firefighters were packing up to leave. This was his dream's way of saying that if he didn't take action soon, it would be too late, and he would lose everything. The fact that the fire was not a fire at all, but a false alarm, tells us that Tom's ambiguous *should I stay* or *should I go* feelings were returning. In other words, when Tom thought there was an immediate threat that he would lose his wife and family, he wanted to fight it with all of his power. Then when he learned that it really wasn't that serious, he began to think he still had time to make a decision about staying or going. By not going into the house to check on his family, his dream revealed that he was trying to divest his emotions from his decision.

The only remaining mystery concerning Tom's dreams was their origin. It is possible that Tom's dreams were simply there to provide a release valve for his immense anxiety. In this scenario, it is possible that God had nothing whatsoever to do with his dreams.

On the other hand, given the circumstances in which Tom came to church and ultimately revealed his dreams, a compelling case could be made that God needed to get Tom's attention and had a few tricks up His sleeve to get it. At the time that I met with Tom, I honestly saw this as a 50/50 proposition. In either event Tom was confronting the problem.

An interesting side note to Tom's dream struck me several days after we'd met. To be honest, these symbols caused me to consider it even more plausible that God had orchestrated Tom's dreams or was seizing the moment to work on him. Let me explain.

A relatively common connotation for water among religious people is baptism. But because Tom wasn't religious, I may have missed this connection the first time. Here's how his dream may represent a more spiritual origin. Tom's dream presented a theme of fire, right? Fire often denotes hell in the dreams of religious people. Therefore, it wouldn't be a stretch to assert that Tom's dream was about his life becoming a living hell.

Since he was a firefighter, Tom's dream featured him rushing around trying to put the fire out with water (baptism), which was where the fire hose symbol entered. Remember that Tom was rushing toward the fire (his life) with a fire hose, which contained the type of water (baptism) that could put the fires of hell out. Therefore, the ultimate symbol to discern was the fire hose because it represented how the baptism water got to the fire. The answer is that the only way to get water on the fire was through Jesus, by becoming a believer. This connection supported the theory that God authored Tom's dreams.

CASE NOTES:

The Dream Message from a Departed Pastor

NAME: Brian
AGE: 32
OCCUPATION: Dentist (church elder)
MARITAL STATUS: Married, with 2 children
(ages 6 and 4)

Whenever I teach classes on the scriptural foundation of dreams, I always leave some time for questions or dream interpretations at the end. That was the case on a hot and humid Sunday in July. I had just concluded a half-day seminar, including meeting individually with a dozen or so people with private dream questions, when I noticed a man seated in the back of the room. As the last person left, I made eye contact with the man, smiled, and asked if it was a good time to answer his dream question.

Smiling back an uneasy smile, the man rose from his chair and admitted there was a dream he wanted clarification on. I promised to do my best and encouraged him to share it.

Brian started by saying that as an elder of a church, he was very uncomfortable coming to a discussion on dreams and even more uncomfortable asking the question he was about to ask.

Having encountered similar sentiments before, I asked, "You don't really buy into psychology or the subject of dreams, right?"

"You could say that," Brian answered with a grin.

"Then what kind of therapist would I be if I didn't ask what in heaven's name brought you to my class?" I teased lightly.

Struggling to get started, Brian explained that he had experienced a dream that had disturbed him greatly. Since he knew I was coming to hold a seminar, he thought perhaps God was using this instance as an opportunity for me to clarify his dream.

I told him I would be honored if God would use me in such a manner and asked him to describe his dream.

"Okay," he answered. "First of all, you know that we lost our senior pastor about a year ago, right?"

"Yes," I replied. "I know he was a great guy and a tremendous spiritual leader in the community. I also recall that he was a pretty good athlete."

"That's him," Brian announced with a hint of pride. "Pastor Davis was a great man who loved to be around his congregation—especially with the guys through sports. That was sort of his special ministry, which made it both particularly difficult and appropriate that he had a heart attack and passed away in the gym right after a men's fellowship basketball game."

Directing Brian back to his dream, I inquired, "Did you have a dream involving Pastor Davis?"

"Yes, I did," he replied. "It's been over a year, and I've not had one dream about Pastor Davis—that is, until the other night. But, Doctor, the interesting thing about my dream is that a couple of other men in our group had a similar—if not the same—dream about Pastor Davis on or about the night I had mine."

If Brian's account was correct, what he was describing is generally accepted as being not only a divinely inspired dream but also what is termed a *broadcast dream*. Broadcast dreams are shared at approximately the same time by two or more people. Broadcast dreams derived their name from the fact that they act something like a radio broadcast. For example, everywhere we go in the world there are broadcast frequencies carrying radio signals, but only people whose radios are tuned in to the right frequency receive the broadcast.

The few reports of broadcast dreams tend to come from Christian missionaries living abroad. Needless to say, they are almost unheard of in the U.S. These reports usually involve as few as two and as many as twenty non-Christians who receive nearly identical dreams. These dreams usually communicate a theme of Christ's love with an invitation to accept Jesus. Most, if not all, secular psychologists pass off this phenomenon as mass suggestion and hysteria.

Without cluing Brian in on what I was thinking, I knew that it was important to determine whether these dreams were divinely sent or a case of mass suggestion. I asked Brian to relay his dream to me.

"Well, as you may know, last week, the church board approved and appointed our new pastor, Pastor Chuck, to the position of senior pastor. In anticipation of that, several of the elders got together Friday. We decided to fast and pray over the weekend. We asked God to provide Pastor Chuck with a smooth transition and his full acceptance by the congregation."

"I understand," I replied. "So tell me about the dream you had."

"Well, my dream takes place in the church gym. The congregation was seated on the bleachers, and Pastor Chuck was preaching a Sunday service from a podium at center court. Then the gym doors opened, and white clouds billowed in. When the clouds cleared, we saw Pastor Davis standing at the doorway. He didn't say anything, but clearly he was smiling as he looked around at the congregation seated on the bleachers. After a moment, he walked up to the podium where Pastor Chuck was preaching, but he still didn't say anything. He just stood behind him, smiling at the congregation and at Pastor Chuck. After a few minutes, he turned and walked from the podium to the gym door. Then just before he walked out of the gym, he turned around, smiled, and disappeared," Brian concluded.

"This is a very important question, Brian, so take a moment if you need it. What sense or overall feeling did you receive during and immediately after your dream?" I inquired.

"Do you mean, was I scared or happy or angry?" he replied. "That type of feeling?"

"Exactly. Was it pleasant or unpleasant?"

"Oh, it was extremely pleasant," he responded. "It was actually a lovely feeling to see him again, and it was a very peaceful dream."

"So tell me how you became aware that some of the others had had a similar dream," I said.

"Well, at first I thought it was just one man, Joe, who'd had the dream. We got together for coffee the other morning, and I told him about my dream in passing. He turned white as a sheet and told me he had exactly the same dream the night after mine, although he remembered a bit more detail than I did."

"What sort of details?" I asked.

"Well, it's sort of silly, but he recalled that Pastor Davis had on his special Fourth of July tie. It had the Stars and Stripes on it and was completely tacky. Everyone kidded him about it and he knew it was tacky, but he wore it only when he was preaching on an Independence Day or Memorial Day weekend. It was kind of a joke between the pastor and the congregation. Kind of a silly but sweet thing, you know?" he explained.

"I understand exactly," I replied. "But you didn't notice that he was wearing his special tie?"

"No, I'm actually surprised I remembered anything about the dream at all," he responded. "My wife would tell you that I don't dream at all, or I just don't remember my dreams. This was very special, though."

"How many of the men in your group who were fasting and praying about the transition have you spoken with about your dream?" I asked.

"Counting my friend, three of us had virtually the same dream. And when I say virtually, I mean each dream took place in the gym, Pastor Chuck was preaching, and Pastor Davis came in smiling but said nothing." He continued, "The only variations were minor, although interesting, like the tie."

"Such as?" I inquired.

"Such as the description of the clouds that he came out of, what he was wearing, and how long he stayed, but the main points were all consistent. So what do you make of it?" he asked pensively.

Pausing to gather my thoughts, I said, "Assuming that all of this is true and that the others aren't just going along with your dream out of support or whatever, this is one of the most conclusive accounts of a broadcast dream I've heard. It passes the first test of a divinely inspired broadcast dream because it happened to a group of religiously sensitive people who were sharing a common purpose. Let me explain. Because you and your group were praying and fasting for your new pastor, each one was in a spiritually similar situation. You availed yourselves of God's leading by asking Him to guide you in helping your new pastor to adapt to his new role and your congregation to feel a part of the transition. In short, you were each acting like a radio tuned in to the same frequency. If the theory holds, then God simply chose to broadcast His message to those of you who were tuned in.

"Your dream symbols were very pronounced and clear," I continued. "The fact that your newly appointed pastor was preaching in the gym and not the sanctuary is full of symbolism. That's likely because at least in your mind and the minds of your colleagues, the gym is the domain of your dearly departed senior pastor. It's also symbolic that your new pastor wasn't preaching in the sanctuary. This is akin to the idea that nobody can fill his shoes.

"Also connected to the gym was that your new pastor was preaching from center court. I would construe this to mean that he was 'holding court,' or he was in charge and was standing at center stage. All of these are connotations of his preaching from the center of the gym floor. I would not discount a sports analogy as a possible dream symbol, either. Consider what goes on at center court in a basketball game." I paused, looking at Brian.

"You mean the jump ball?" he answered.

"Precisely, and jump ball means that the ball—or prize—is up for grabs. In this situation, that could mean *it's anybody's call.* In other words, no one knew for sure how the new pastor was going to replace your senior pastor, but it seems to have worked out.

"Now, let's take a look at the fact that when the doors opened, clouds billowed in, and your pastor was standing at the doorway smiling, yet silent."

"Yes," Brian quickly interrupted, "that's the part that has us all confused. Why didn't he speak and just tell us this was God's will?"

"Wonderful question," I complimented him. "If you look at the way God used dreams to communicate throughout the Bible, you'll see that He didn't always spell it out that easily. I will, however, tell you what I think it means. I think the fact that your senior pastor entered the gym through the doors tells us that he has a new church home—that is, heaven—although he is still very connected to your church and congregation. The billowing clouds don't require a doctorate degree to decipher. They are a dream symbol denoting heaven and suggesting that he's merely visiting."

"And there's nothing odd about him just smiling? Does it mean he was happy?" Brian asked.

"I think you are right on target," I replied, much to his encouragement. "The way you describe it, I get a vision that he entered smiling and walked to a position at center court, but behind your new pastor. It's important to note that he chose to stand behind. He could have shared the pulpit, stood off to the side, or stood directly in front for that matter. The old pastor standing behind the new pastor makes me think of a gesture of support and encouragement. And as for his smile, I get a feeling it was the smile of a proud or satisfied father who was pleased with something his children did. Are you following?" I asked.

"Yes!" Brian exclaimed.

"Then in your dream, your senior pastor sensed all was well, and left through the same doorway to heaven from which he arrived, still smiling," I concluded.

"That makes sense to me, but what about the small differences some of us noted in our dreams?" he asked. "For instance, two saw his Fourth of July tie, and I didn't. What does that mean?"

I explained to him there are subtle differences that always seem to filter into dreams that more than one person has received. Just as people see things differently when they are awake, so they do in their sleep. When I was in the police academy, they trained us by staging crimes right in front of our eyes. Then they would tell us to write a police report based on the facts we had observed. Most of us would come up with reports that were basically the same, but there would always be officers who saw just a little bit more or a little bit less. It was a condition of their powers of observation and memory. I went on to discuss how the same factor appeared true in broadcast dreams. Some see every detail while others catch only the main points.

"Would it then be safe to say that none of us are psychotic?" Brian said with a laugh.

"I don't know if I'd climb that far out on the limb, Brian," I answered in jest. "But on a serious note, I think what you and the others experienced is an amazing gift from God. It's possible, maybe even likely, that you will never encounter a similar situation. You should take great comfort and joy in knowing that God was tuned in to you and you were tuned in to God at the same time. It's also safe to say Pastor Davis is quite satisfied with Pastor Chuck and how the church is dealing with the transition."

EPILOGUE

I found Brian's dream completely believable and verifiable through the other members of his group, each of whom was fasting and praying for their church and their new pastor. As is often the case with broadcast dreams, this one did not return. And at the time of my writing this dream account, Brian related that all is well at his church and there has been a smooth transition between pastors.

Certainly skeptics and atheists would disagree vehemently with my assertion that Brian and the elders actually experienced a divinely inspired dream. They would point to any number of coincidental rationales behind a similar dream reaching several individuals on the same day or close to it. I would respectfully disagree. After careful consideration, I believe this dream accurately describes a divinely inspired broadcast dream. I base this conclusion on the following facts:

1. More than one of the elders experienced nearly, if not exactly, the same dream.

2. The elders experienced the dream on or about the same day.

3. The elders were actively seeking God's direction through fasting and prayer at the time.

4. Their dream was consistent with all they knew and understood about God's nature.

5. Each one had peace and calmness about the dream and the transition between pastors.

It was a privilege to encounter such a dream. It did strike me as ironic that a spiritual group of men would get together and pray and fast for God's leading and then shy away from the possibility that God chose to honor their prayers in dreams. I had to fight the urge to overanalyze the psychology behind these spiritual men's cycle of seek–find–doubt. I think there is perhaps an easier explanation. God created mankind with a discounting and doubting nature. The Gospels provide us with example after example of how people were confronted with the Truth, in human form, and yet discounted and denied His credibility. If nothing else, this illustrates just how far Christians have come from understanding God's sovereignty over all matters—including dreams.

I also have found that common, household embarrassment plays a role in dream skepticism among believers. It's one thing to announce, "Boy, I've been praying about this, and God has finally given me peace about it." It's quite another thing to say, "Boy, did I ever appreciate the fact that God visited me in my dream last night and revealed how I should handle this situation." There's a fear that half our friends would roll their eyes and the other half would casually suggest Prozac. We've so conditioned ourselves to accept that God comes to us through a narrow pipeline that forcing our minds to explore a different avenue of connectivity is often the last thing we consider and, even then, are quick to discount.

CASE NOTES:

The Silver-Plated Dream

NAME: Ron
AGE: 61
OCCUPATION: Senior pastor
MARITAL STATUS: Married 14 years

R on, a senior pastor at a charismatic church, called my receptionist requesting an appointment in two weeks. Ron did so because he resides out of state and wanted to take advantage of lower airfares. When asked about the nature of his appointment, Ron told my receptionist that he had been experiencing a very disturbing and recurring dream, but that he didn't want to divulge it over the phone—especially to a receptionist, as he put it.

Ron arrived for his appointment and asked that before we started the session, we pray for God's will and the revelation of whether his wife was, in fact, having an affair with a deacon from his church. Just for the record, Ron also prayed that if she was having an affair, God would punish his adulterous wife mightily for her sins. Any way you sliced it, I knew it was going to be an interesting case.

"Ron, I'm not sure we should consume our thoughts with how God will or will not handle something that we don't even know the answer to," I began. "Especially when your suspicions are based on a recurring dream. Let's examine the dreams and then we'll go from there. Okay?"

"I must correct you on your false assumption, my good doctor," Ron said smugly. "I am not basing the infidelity charge against my Mrs. solely on dreams God has given me. I have also visited a—how should I put it?—a magi of sorts." Hesitating, Ron looked at me out of the corner of his eye and sarcastically asked, "You do know what a *magi* is, don't you?"

Biting my lip and thinking to myself that Ron was going to be a royal pain, I replied, "If you mean *magi* as in the fellows consulted by King Herod in Matthew 2, then yes, I do know. In biblical times the word *magi* was used for a variety of types such as magicians, soothsayers, and astrologers. These guys were generally into gathering power through occult practices and trickery."

"You know what?" Ron said. "Before we go further I need to apologize. I mean you no disrespect, and I'm sorry if I am coming across as a jerk!"

"No harm, no foul, Ron," I answered. "This must be a tough time for you. Why don't you tell me about the magi visit?"

"I have a friend who regularly visits an astrologer in a large city near our church. When I told my friend that my wife and I had not been getting along well lately, he apparently took the liberty of seeing his astrologer for a consultation." Leaning back in his chair, Ron continued, "The astrologer told my friend that my wife was having an affair and that it was with someone close to me."

"I understand," I said. "Did you subsequently visit this astrologer?"

"I most certainly did," Ron snapped back defensively. "And you needn't question whether it was proper for a pastor to visit an astrologer, either. In my church, we are open-minded about *all* spiritual things. God created heaven, earth, and all the stars and planets in the universe. Certainly it isn't far-fetched to assume that there must be some pattern or connection to the way they all align."

"And the way the stars and planets align enabled the astrologer to see the past and predict the future?" I asked while mustering all the professionalism I could find to resist the urge to roll my eyes.

"Not so much predict the future, Doctor, but predict trends or possibilities based on the general appearance of the solar system on a given day," Ron asserted.

Ron went on to explain that he was told the stars and planets were aligned in such a manner that over the past eight weeks, Sagittarius, that is, people with his wife's birth date, would be emotionally and sexually vulnerable. He said that had she consulted him, he'd have warned her to stay away from Cancer men because they are the most apt to prey on a Sagittarius in her weakened state.

I probed for specifics the magi had given Ron. He responded by stating that his advisor had told him she was having carnal relations with someone with close ties to Ron's church organization, even describing the man as tall with thinning hair and a mustache. Ron was told that the man pretended to be a friend and confidant, but that he should be wary because the man was not only after Ron's wife, but also after his position as a senior pastor.

I asked him if the description matched anyone Ron was familiar with at church.

"To a tee," Ron smirked as though he'd been let in on an inside joke. "At first I couldn't believe it. Deacon Tim has been a spiritual leader in our church for ten years. He's had dinner with my family, and our families have even gone on vacations together. I actually convinced myself that my astrologer was wrong, but then God spoke to me and confirmed my suspicions through my dreams."

"And what did God reveal to you in your dreams?" I inquired.

"My first dream was sent to me about eight weeks ago," he replied. "In my dream I was with my pastoral staff and elders in a church business meeting. Instead of taking my usual seat at the head of the table, I was standing on top of the large board table, my arms outstretched and waving slightly in an effort to get them to look at me. The people were seated around the table, but they had their backs to me and wouldn't acknowledge me in any way.

"In my dream this upset me to the point that I broke down in tears. I excused myself so I could regain my composure. I walked downstairs and then out into the garden area in back of the sanctuary. That's when I noticed that everyone from the meeting was already outside.

"Then I saw my wife, and she was kneeling next to the fountain. Behind her was Deacon Tim. He was holding her hand, and they were tossing silver dollars into the fountain as though it were a wishing well." Ron added, "They both looked up at me, and I could see that Tim had two silver coins for eyes. My wife and Tim started to laugh, and soon my entire staff began laughing. I was left there at the fountain while my wife, Deacon Tim, and my entire staff turned and walked away."

"I can see how this dream would be distressing, Ron," I consoled him.

"You bet it was distressing, but it was more than just a dream," he announced. "It was God's confirmation to me that my wife is cheating. I would have never taken the action I did, had I just thought this was a silly dream and not a divine vision."

Suspecting the worst, I asked, "What sort of action did you take?"

"Well, I couldn't very well fire my wife, but I sure can fire my deacon."

Dreading where this was going, I asked whether he had confronted the deacon with his evidence from the magi. He assured me that he had, and then he stated that he was appalled at the man's gall. Deacon Tim had the temerity to tell Ron he was aware that Ron's wife was having an affair, but it wasn't with him. The deacon said that she had come to him for advice on how to break off the affair, but he didn't want to get involved.

Ron ended by bursting into bitter laughter. "What a laugh! He tried to tell me he didn't want to get involved while he was actively leading her into hell!" Ron concluded.

"Ron," I asked quietly, "did you talk to your wife about the possibility of an affair?"

Shooting me an annoyed look, Ron replied, "Of course I did. She immediately broke into tears and asked me to forgive her, but she's protecting Tim to the end. She said it wasn't him, but everything else confirms it and I know she's thought of him as attractive because she's told me so!

"WHAT GALL!" Ron shouted so loudly that I'm sure every doctor in the next two buildings heard him. "She tells me that she's been having an affair, that she's really sorry, but then she won't tell me who it is! As if I don't already know who it is!"

"Did you reveal to her that you suspected . . ."

"SUSPECTED?" Ron interrupted. "How can you call it a suspicion when a spiritual advisor tells me that my wife is cheating on me, and then I come to find out that she is cheating on me? The advisor described Deacon Tim to a tee, and then God sent me a dream that Deacon Tim was having carnal relations with my wife. Do you call that suspicion? I call it irrefutable evidence."

In a more subdued tone, Ron stated, "I'm sorry, Doctor. I don't mean to shout, and I'm not mad at you at all. I'm just hurt, frustrated, and alone. I know what happened, but I thought that you would confirm my dream and I'd have total peace of mind when I divorce my wife for adultery."

"I know you're not angry with me, Ron, and no apology is necessary," I responded. "I do have some thoughts about the symbols in your dream.

"Your first symbol of standing on the table in your boardroom, talking with arms outstretched in an effort to get the others to listen, is quite clear," I began.

"Standing on the table represents your pulpit or platform. This is the position of authority from which you preach. Your outstretched arms are also a dream symbol that is unique to religious people. This is symbolic of the crucifixion of Christ. This tells us that your state of mind, at least in this sequence, is that you are speaking from your normal position of authority, but you fear you are being emotionally or professionally crucified. This image is punctuated by the fact that your arms are outstretched, like those of a man being crucified. On the other hand, you are waving your arms—punctuating your protest. This dream symbolism reflects your frustration, even anger, over feeling as though you are being crucified, but no one will come to your rescue.

"In your dream, everyone at the table had his back to you because, in real life, you fear that the church leaders, coworkers, and friends will shun you or turn their backs on you when you reveal what is going on in your personal life.

"Let's continue to the part where you began crying and excused yourself from the meeting," I said. "This suggests that in your waking life, you're uncomfortable with this group seeing this side of you. Perhaps you are worried that they might think you are weak. Maybe you fear a connection that if you can't take care of your own life, they will wonder how you can take care of the church. In essence, Ron, it's a fear of being seen as a failure. Are you still with me?"

"Yes, and I'm in complete agreement with what you're telling me," he replied. "Please proceed."

"On to the dream image that Deacon Tim wasn't a part of the meeting. I need to take care of a timing question first," I stated. "Was the first occasion for this recurring dream series before or after you visited the astrologer?"

Thinking for a moment, Pastor Ron arrived at the decision I had hoped he would. "The dream followed the visit to my spiritual advisor. That's when God supplied the confirmation through my dreams," he concluded.

"Very well. Now let's move on to the dream symbols of the wishing well and of your wife kneeling beside it with the two of them tossing silver dollars into the fountain. A wishing well in a dream often denotes one's hopes and wishes. Certainly in this case it is your hope and wish that this is not happening. It also may connect to the biblical account of the woman caught in adultery who was being accused by the Pharisees [John 8:1–6]."

Continuing, I interpreted the meaning behind the deacon's eyes, which appeared as two silver coins in the pastor's dream: "This is a very unusual dream symbol, and I wonder if it doesn't connect to your belief that someone close to you has turned on you. I know you're familiar with how Judas betrayed Jesus for thirty silver coins [Matt. 27:3]. So, if this theory is on target, this represents how you believe Deacon Tim is a Judas in that he betrayed your confidence.

"You should also understand," I said with a hint of caution in my voice, "that in the secular, humanistic world of dream interpretation, eyes mean a wide variety of things like windows to the soul, love, flirting, or flattery. Every dream dictionary I've ever read attaches some romantic or odd and mysterious connotation to the appearance of eyes in a dream. Let me clarify this from a Christian and biblical position. I've encountered somewhere between two and three hundred dreams from Christians or religious-minded people who have seen eyes as dream symbols. I've found that the vast majority represent a desire to seek revenge."

"What do you mean, revenge?" he asked.

"Let's play a little Bible word trivia," I said. "What is the most common scripture connected with the word *eye?*"

"I think," he said, pausing, "I think of Exodus and Moses' statement about revenge, 'eye for eye, tooth for tooth' [Ex. 21:24] and so on."

"Exactly," I replied. "That's exactly where most Christians go when they associate the word *eye* with a Bible verse. This leads me to believe that there are two dream symbols layered one on top of the other. The first silver coin symbol over the deacon's eyes denotes betrayal, while the second denotes a desire for revenge."

"I beg to differ with you, Doctor," he stated sharply. "I am a man of God, and I am not the type who seeks revenge."

"I'm sorry, Pastor," I said with a slight edge of sarcasm, "I must have misunderstood. I thought you told me you already fired the deacon."

"No, you heard me correctly," he snapped back. "I wasn't about to have a man of his character in an advisory role in my church. What would you have had me do in that situation?" he asked.

Gathering my thoughts, I admitted that I would have counseled him to be sure of his facts before acting and also suggested that he not rely on a "spiritual advisor" followed by a dream for such major decisions. He could only stammer a weak reply and restate that God had confirmed his suspicions through the dream and that such a fact could not be discounted.

"Pastor, I'm not at all sure your dreams are confirmation from God," I observed. "In fact, if you were to pin me down to one position or the other, I'd have to say I believe the dream was not divinely inspired, but a manifestation brought on by the anxiety this whole situation has caused you."

"And what do you base that on?" he demanded.

"On the fact that you told me that you started having the dreams *after* you visited your 'spiritual advisor' and not before. In cases where evidence points to God's active involvement in providing a dream, I don't see Him waiting for a fortune-teller, psychic, tarot card reader, or astrologer to open the door," I said resolutely. "To sum it up, Pastor, God moves first, not second behind worldly magi."

Pausing for a moment to allow Ron to cool down, I said, "Let me ask you one final question, which is often the litmus test for determining whether a dream is divinely or personally inspired. After you fired Deacon Tim, did your dreams change or go away?"

Pastor Ron closed his eyes to ponder the question before replying, "Well, no. And to be honest with you, I thought they would since I had rid my life and organization of a cancer!"

"Then ask yourself this question," I continued. "If the situation were just as you believed it to be, that is, your wife was sorry and asked for forgiveness and you only needed to rid your life of the deacon, then why hasn't God discontinued the dream? After all, if the dream was His way of warning you to take action, then you've done exactly that. The case should be closed. Let me provide you with the only possible defense as to why God may continue to send you these dreams. It's possible that you still have so much anxiety over this situation that the dreams aren't going away," I said while not providing him with time to respond.

"If I may ask, Pastor, has Deacon Tim appeared in dreams other than the ones we've discussed?"

"Well, yes. I have had a couple of dreams about him, but that's only natural given what he's done, isn't it?" he asked.

"As I said, that's possible," I replied. "Can you recall any of them?"

"I do recall bits and pieces of one dream involving Tim that I've had a couple of times recently. The only thing I can remember of my dream is that we had driven together to a pastors' retreat and it was snowing. Tim was in one cabin and I was in another," he recounted. Then he asked, "What do you make of that?"

"That's a no-brainer," I responded. "The pastors' conference represented the professional relationship the two of you have had. You had driven to it together, which denotes a closer than professional relationship. Because you two were in separate cabins, your dream was acknowledging that there was considerable emotional distance between you. But the clincher is the snow. Snow nearly always represents frozen emotions or a clean start." I paused. "So the quick summary of this dream is that you are feeling emotionally cut off from Deacon Tim and may be secretly desiring a clean start."

In a serious tone I added, "Let me make one point very clear, though, Pastor. I don't know whether or not the deacon had an affair with your wife. He says no and she says no. The only remote evidence that it *was* the deacon comes from a generic description your 'spiritual advisor' gave you, a dream, and a statement your wife made that she thinks Deacon Tim is attractive. It's entirely plausible that your dreams are not at all confirmation from God, but continued anxiety over your wife's affair and the possibility that you fired the wrong guy."

Pastor Ron sat back in his chair and was still for the first time in the session.

Seizing the opportunity to try to send the pastor away with a constructive plan, I stated, "You may just want to do yourself, your wife, Deacon Tim, and your church a huge favor and think clearly through this situation. I know you're in prayer over it, but at least be open to the possibility that you have allowed a jealous imagination to fan a fire that was started by your 'spiritual advisor.' I also strongly urge you and your wife to get into counseling so that, at the least, you can get some closure and prepare to move on in life."

EPILOGUE

Earlier I mentioned how a high number of religious people associate the word *eye* with the Old Testament passage found in Exodus 21:24. In actuality, 73 percent of Christians associated the word *eye* with this famous "eye for eye, tooth for tooth" passage. To complete the thought regarding the second most commonly associated scripture with the word *eye*, 21 percent of Christians cited Matthew 18:9. This is where Jesus issues a warning about being drawn into sin by admonishing that if your eye causes you to sin, gouge it out and throw it away.

We've established how the secular world often views dream symbols through an entirely different prism. The vast majority of dream interpretation manuals I have collected over the years refer to eyes as a dream symbol by trying to make distinctions based on color of eyes, closed versus open eyes, and the like. Then in typical New Age fashion, they try to predict some future event: for example, if you dream of green eyes, you will likely come into money. This is a prime example of why secular dream symbols and the accompanying books have little or no relevance to Christians.

In regard to Pastor Ron and his scenario, about four weeks after our initial visit, I received a phone update. He told me that he took my advice and that he and his wife were in marital counseling with an eye (no pun intended) on reconciliation. In their second counseling session his wife revealed that her affair had not been with Deacon Tim, but someone else on the pastoral staff at the church. The pastor did not volunteer, nor did I ask for, the details.

The pastor added that he understood my reluctance to accept what his "spiritual advisor" had seen, but that I should try to keep a more open mind. He maintained the accuracy of his astrologer in describing the adulterous man. That is, except for the mustache. It seems the man his wife was having an affair with did not have a mustache. The pastor was able to clear up that inconsistency by noting that the man did, in fact, wear a mustache earlier in his life. One can only surmise that the psychic must have received an old mental image.

On a final note, and just to clarify any confusion. I did not—nor do I now—condone consulting astrologers, magi, tea-leaf readers, palm readers, or the like. I view them as anti-scriptural and evidence that those who need them do not have a truly trusting relationship with Jesus grounded in the belief that He is enough.

CASE NOTES:

The Abortion Clinic Nightmare

NAME: Rory
AGE: 27
OCCUPATION: Police officer
MARITAL STATUS: Married 4 years, with 1 child (age 2)

A n old adage among police officers is that there are only two types of people—cops and noncops. Perhaps that, more than any other reason, explains why I always seemed to have a half dozen or more police officers, or their families, coming to me for counseling. As a retired cop, I have sensitivity to the unique issues affecting their lives.

One such case involved a police officer referred to me by his department for what is commonly referred to as PTSD, or post-traumatic stress disorder. As a diagnosis, post-traumatic stress disorder really wasn't known until Vietnam veterans returned from the war. Those who saw particularly shocking and stressful action often appeared fine for weeks, months, and even years, but later they developed symptoms of severe depression or anxiety. Many of these cases resulted in suicidal or homicidal tendencies, so as a result, this diagnosis is taken very seriously. Police officers and emergency workers, because of the nature of their professions, are profoundly susceptible to PTSD.

In our initial visit, Rory told me that he had been fighting severe anxiety since he was involved as a SWAT team hostage negotiator in a situation that resulted in the shooting of a suspect who had taken over a medical clinic. Rory's anxiety displayed itself in the form of panic attacks whereby he would hyperventilate (panic accompanied by uncontrollable rapid breathing) and become light-headed for seemingly no reason whatsoever. I learned that Rory had also been experiencing a recurring nightmare for a little more than three months. He had been to the department psychologist for counseling and then to a psychiatrist, who prescribed a common antianxiety medication. Because Rory was on medication, he was removed from street duty and assigned to the front desk, which is also referred to as "policeman purgatory" because it is the most boring assignment there is.

It's a good thing first impressions aren't everything because I'd have wagered that Rory and I would not do particularly well. At least that's the first thing I remember about our initial session. He came fifteen minutes late, dressed shabbily in cutoff jeans and a police academy sweatshirt that looked as if it predated WWII.

Greeting me with a very limp handshake, he slouched into my couch, displaying all the enthusiasm of a high school football player in a sewing class. Offering no reason for his tardiness, he lay back and closed his eyes.

"So, Rory . . . what brings you into my happy, happy world?" I said, reverting to my old cop sarcasm. Rory remained motionless, lying on his back with his right arm resting over his eyes. Refusing to take the bait that Rory was floating past me, I said, "Do me a favor. I'm going to step into the outer office and catch up on some reading. If you get tired of trying to pull my chain, give me a holler and I'll come back in and we can chat, okay?"

About ten minutes passed before Rory opened the door to the outer office and poked his head around the corner. "Sorry for being a jerk," he said. "I'm just getting a little bit tired of seeing doctors. No offense?"

I nodded, and we headed back into my office. After some small talk designed to let Rory know that I wasn't the enemy and could actually relate to him on the "cop" level as well as on the level of a therapist, I delved into the circumstances that led to his problems and asked him about the hostage situation.

With a sigh he explained fairly swiftly what had happened. Their SWAT team was assigned to handle a takeover situation at a family planning clinic. Some wacko religious fanatic had barged into the clinic and chased out all the patients waiting for their abortions. Then the suspect decided he would teach the doctor and his nurse assistant a lesson in Christian love and forgiveness. Rory's team responded, and the snipers and entry teams took their positions as Rory became the negotiator.

"My SWAT team commander chose me because he knows I'm a Christian, or was a Christian, so he figured I'd have the best chance of dealing with a religious nutcase. I got on the phone with him, and we started this really crazy dialogue," he concluded.

I wasn't sure what "crazy dialogue" entailed, so I asked for an example.

"I mean, this guy was yelling and screaming that the day of God's wrath had come and that God had appointed him to lead in the Rapture by killing all the baby killers first."

"Which was why he started at the abortion clinic?" I asked.

"Precisely," he replied. "So there I was, trying to talk this wacko out of killing the doctor and his nurse, and the nutcase asked me a question that caused him to go off."

"What question did he ask?" I inquired.

"At first he was quoting me the Bible as his source of direction in taking out the doc and his nurse. I told him that God wouldn't do that and that he must have misunderstood God's message. He sort of paused and was thinking, and then he asked me if I was a Christian," Rory said while looking up at the ceiling.

"I told him that I was a Christian and that's why I knew that God wouldn't want him to kill anyone. Then I told him that I wanted to help get him out of the jam he was in.

"That's when he softened a little and told me his name: Joshua. Figures it would be a biblical name, doesn't it? Anyway, I thought I was making headway until he stated that if I was really a brother in Christ and not an agent of Satan, then he would be willing to discuss Esther 8:11 with me. I told him I didn't have a Bible with me, and he almost flipped right then and there. Then it went downhill fast."

I asked for clarification: "What do you mean by downhill, Rory?"

"I mean, he started drilling me to see if I knew my Bible and if I was really a Christian," he replied.

"That was a no-win situation, to say the least," I acknowledged. "How did you handle it?"

Speaking slowly, but clearly becoming agitated, Rory explained how the man had claimed God had warned him that there would be demons sent to stop him and that he was supposed to test these demons about certain areas of the Bible. The suspect had asked Rory to tell him what books of the Bible preceded and followed the book of Esther. Rory couldn't remember and was getting more agitated all the time.

"Then it came down to an ultimatum," Rory continued. "He told me that if I were a Christian, then I could tell him the chapter and verse where God says, 'An eye for an eye.' He said that if I could tell him where that's found in the Bible, he'd see that as a sign from God and put his gun down and come out.

"My brain was racing. Was it Exodus or Genesis? I was so confused that I started to wonder if it was something Jesus said in the New Testament. He just kept pressing me, and I kept stalling, trying to think and trying to give the SWAT team time. Finally I stalled long enough, and the entry team went in and killed Josh . . . the suspect."

Leaning forward in my chair, I softly asked whether Rory was assuming responsibility for the suspect's death. Obviously he felt that if he had known his Bible backward and forward, he would have given the suspect the answers he was looking for, and the suspect would have given up.

Rory's sarcastic wit came back as he replied, "You're a quick study, Doc. But it's the blasted nightmares I keep having—at least three times a week—that are driving me insane."

Sensing the opening I'd been looking for to connect, I asked if he wanted to unburden himself of the recurring nightmare.

He agreed, saying that I might as well get a turn inside his brain since everyone else had taken a turn already.

"I thought it was feeling a bit crowded." I gave him back the sarcasm before we began.

"After you've awakened from your dream," I queried, "what is your emotional state—that is, are you confused, troubled, angry, or elated?"

After thinking a moment, Rory replied, "I wake up shaking like a leaf, and I've usually sweated right through my pajamas. I'm completely terrified, but I'm confused too."

"That's amazing," I said, looking serious.

"What's amazing?" he quizzed. "What are you thinking?"

Trying to keep a straight face, I replied, "I didn't think cops ever slept in pajamas."

"Oh, that's great," he declared. "Hundreds of comedy writers out on strike, and I get the only one who doubles as a shrink. Okay, you got me. May I continue?"

"Please do, and I'll try to contain myself," I said, sensing that Rory and I were connecting on a level that would help us work more closely.

In a serious tone, Rory began relating his dream: "I was a cop in my dream, but I didn't work for my police department. I wore a black police uniform with a red badge. I went around from city to city searching for something, but I didn't know what it was. Every hospital I came to I started looking through patient rooms for pregnant women. The rooms were all the same, with four walls and a door, but no ceiling, which allowed this police helicopter to hover above me with a spotlight directing me from room to room.

"Then, even though I was inside different hospitals, I always seemed to find this one particular patient room. I stood outside the door with my gun drawn, and I could hear voices inside. They knew I was in the hospital, but they didn't know I was standing right outside the door preparing to kill them all. I couldn't stand them talking about me anymore, so I broke the door down and charged inside. I looked up, and I felt the white-hot searchlight from the police helicopter, which was now directly overhead."

Taking a moment to gather his thoughts, Rory continued, "Then I noticed the pregnant woman in bed. She was surrounded by three doctors and her husband, but none of them noticed me because they were all looking at her chart. Instead of using my gun, I pulled out a long butcher knife and walked to her bed and leaned down and kissed her on the cheek. Then I took my knife and plunged it into her stomach three times while the others in the room just watched. Then a bullet was fired from the white light of the police helicopter. It struck me in the brain and dropped me like a sack of potatoes. I pulled myself up to a seated position, and there was blood running out of my mouth. I couldn't speak, and nobody would lift a hand to help me. They all just watched me die."

As he concluded his nightmare account, I could tell that Rory was breathing rapidly and appeared close to having a panic attack. I told him to lean forward and put his head between his knees and think about the happiest thing he could think of. A moment passed, and Rory straightened and thanked me before asking me what I thought of his dream.

"I have to give your brain credit, Rory," I said. "That's one vivid imagination driving your nightmare. It's pretty transparent, though."

He encouraged me to work my magic, so I continued, "You've got to look at the recurring symbols in your nightmare and connect them with the real-life events that have caused you to have the panic attacks. Let's look first at the fact that you *are* a cop in your dream, but you *don't* work for your department. These symbols tell us that you're still a policeman at heart, but you feel separated, unneeded, and unwanted by your own department.

"Then in your dream, you're wearing black clothing and a red badge. You don't need to be a dream detective to understand that wearing black means you're a bad guy," I related. "It's the red badge that interests me the most. What's the first image that pops into your head when I say red?" I asked.

"I don't know," he replied. "Maybe *red* devil or *red* blood."

"Yeah, that's exactly where I was. My hunch is that you are wearing black because you are not one of the good guys anymore, and you are wearing a red badge because you are working for Satan . . . in your dream, of course," I concluded.

Rory nodded his assent and waited to hear more.

Continuing the unraveling of his dream, I called his attention to the hospital and his frantic search: "Rory, I don't think I've ever heard a more fascinating version of the birth of Christ."

"What are you talking about?" he stammered. "You've lost it."

"Perhaps, but I'm sure about this one," I explained. "Let me show you. You are wandering from hospital to hospital in search of a pregnant woman. You are directed to just the right hospital and the right room, or manger if you prefer, by a light from above. And just in case you're starting to discount my theory that the light from the helicopter is actually the star out of the East that directed the three wise men to the baby Jesus in Matthew 2:10, then take a look at who was in the hospital room. Three doctors, aka three wise men; the pregnant woman, aka the Virgin Mary; and her husband, aka Joseph. Can I get an amen?" I asked.

"Not yet, but go ahead. I'm still with you."

I unraveled the symbols, explaining in particular the tremendous significance of what happened to the pregnant woman, or the Virgin Mary. Rory had kissed her on the cheek in his dream and then killed her. I drew his attention to the Bible and the ultimate betrayer's kiss on the cheek of Jesus. I led Rory to examine what happened to Judas after he kissed Jesus on the cheek and left with the silver.

"He died, Doc. Oh, wow! I see myself as a Judas?" he asked.

I nodded and encouraged him to proceed with the rest of the dream in order to deal with it fully. My next conclusions involved the three stabbing motions Rory performed in his dream. It is plausible that he stabbed her three times to represent three deaths: the Father, Son, and Holy Spirit.

"Next, you are shot through the head from the white light above, which denotes your perception that *God* was the One who killed you. The fact that you were shot through the brain belies your perception that God has killed you for your lack of brains. Finally you slumped to the floor, bleeding from the mouth and unable to speak. This final string of symbols tells us how you perceive your relationship with God. You perceive God is literally through with you, so He is taking your life. You perceive He is doing so because you are stupid. And you can't speak, so there is no way to appeal to God for mercy. In other words, it's hopeless," I added.

Rory's whole dream was about his subconscious feelings of guilt and shame that he betrayed God. He believed he let God down by not being able to recite a specific chapter and verse from the Bible. His dream pointed to his guilty feelings that he was responsible for the suspect's death in the family planning clinic.

Rory sat transfixed without speaking for a few minutes.

Finally I said, "I know I've tossed a lot of information your way in a very short period of time. Everything you're feeling is exactly how I'd have felt if I'd had to deal with what you've gone through. Rory, that suspect elected through his own free will to take over that family planning clinic. God could have intervened, but He allows all of us to choose to do right or to do wrong. It was the suspect's choice to die in the clinic or to give up. He chose to die. You didn't choose for him."

I concluded the session by reminding Rory of one of my favorite pieces of Scripture: "Look, I don't want this to sound like a Sunday school class, but Romans 8:28 applies here. It says, 'In all things God works for the good of those who love him, who have been called according to his purpose.' That means that God uses circumstances like these for a greater purpose. If you bail on Him, then you've stuck a wrench in the spokes of His plan. The event is in the past, and your task now is to find out what good God has planned and what your part is in His plan."

Epilogue

Rory continued to come for sessions for about two months. Only once during that period did he have a similar nightmare, but it wasn't as severe, and he effectively dealt with it. His psychiatrist discontinued his medication, and he returned to full, active duty.

About six months later, I received a letter from Rory telling me that he believed the recurring nightmare was God's way of getting his attention. He also concluded that part of the message was that a professing Christian should have the scriptural knowledge to back it up. Or as he put it, if you're going to walk the walk, you'd better be able to talk the talk.

He also prayerfully concluded that God wanted more of his life than he could give while serving in law enforcement. As a result, in his off time Rory enrolled at seminary with the goal of becoming a pastor. His long-term vision was a ministry with runaway teens and unwed mothers.

CASE NOTES:

God Confirms a Mission

NAME: Eric
AGE: 36
OCCUPATION: Missionary
MARITAL STATUS: Married 12 years, with 2 children
(ages 9 and 7)

I have a vexing question regarding dreams that given the luxury, I would love to ask God. The question concerns why non-American Christians, and even American Christians in foreign missionary service, seem to have divine dreams with some regularity. Often I hear accounts of American missionaries who never had a divine dream while in the States having one or many upon entering the mission field. For now, my theory is that once Christians make the additional commitment of faith that it takes to be a foreign missionary, it opens them up to a heightened experiential relationship with God.

This story illustrates this point. I had finished speaking about dreams and visions at a large church when a missionary who had just returned from six years in India approached me. He introduced himself as Eric and told me that he was particularly interested in my seminar because of all the spiritual dreams he and other missionaries encounter abroad.

Eric and I discussed my theory about why there are so many more spiritual dreams among American-born missionaries and relatively few among American-born Christians who aren't missionaries. Eric had a second theory, which was that American-born Christians take religious freedom for granted.

In countries where committing your soul to Christ can land you in jail or worse, choosing to become a Christian is not a cavalier undertaking. People make such a decision at the cost of great self-sacrifice, such as facing rejection by their family, friends, and employers.

Conversely Americans who become Christians often do so with relative ease. They may have to abandon worldly friends and distracting lifestyles, but their lives are seldom in jeopardy. Eric's theory is that this creates a different breed of Christian, one who perhaps doesn't experience the commitment to Christ that comes from a "baptism under fire."

Eric also theorized that missionaries encounter more divine dreams among foreign, born-again Christians because they are straining for God in every aspect of their lives. Again, when you make a decision that will alter your relationship with your family and friends and that could land you in jail, you tend to seek God's guidance with a magnifying glass.

Eric's case in point came about eight weeks prior to our discussion, just before his return to America. Since he was an American missionary in India, Eric's activities were often closely monitored. Muslims who make the choice to denounce their religion and follow Jesus are subjected to punishment ranging from beatings and public humiliation to shunning from families and friends. It stands to reason that missionaries who encourage such conversions are not particularly welcome—even in *free* countries.

When Eric was serving food to the poor in what is Nepal's equivalent to a soup kitchen, he met Rajak. Rajak spoke English and seemed to connect with Eric, who routinely talked about Jesus during and after his shift at the shelter. As was often his custom, Eric offered to pray the Sinner's Prayer with any in the group who wanted to accept Jesus as their personal Lord and Savior. Although interested in learning more about Jesus, Rajak could not bring himself to make that fateful commitment at that time.

Weeks later, Rajak made the long trek from his hometown back to Nepal to look up Eric. Finding him at the soup kitchen, Rajak told Eric that he must have a moment of his time after his dinner shift to share an odd recurring dream he had been having. Eric agreed and asked Rajak to meet him in back of the shelter after an hour. When the two got together, Eric could see that Rajak was both nervous and excited at the prospect of trying to learn more about his odd dream, which he readily shared with Eric.

He had been traveling along a dry riverbed that ran between his home and Nepal. Rajak explained that he had walked this riverbed for years, and it never had water in it. But in his dream, one day he was heading home from Nepal, and even though it hadn't rained for months, the river began to fill with what appeared to be water. The water came past Rajak's knees, beginning to form a strong current. It then turned to blood and continued to rise until it was past his waist and had moved up to his chest. He was afraid of drowning if someone didn't help him.

Then he looked at one side of the riverbank and saw all his family and friends. They were calling out to him. He could see their faces, and they were screaming to him, but no sound was coming out of their mouths. They reached out their hands to try to save him from drowning, but for some reason Rajak couldn't reach out for them. Instead, he remained in the river of blood until it covered his head. He found himself lying on his back at the bottom of the river, looking up.

He grew very frightened when he saw several large black fish circling in the water above him. They saw him at the bottom and encircled him. He was running out of air and wanted to get to the surface, but as he tried to swim, the fish formed a barrier and wouldn't let him up. He knew he would drown, and yet he allowed himself to simply float to the bottom to die. That event ended his dream.

Eric told me that he had tried to make some sense of Rajak's dream for him, but he had a limited understanding of dreams and didn't want to confuse or misdirect him. That, he said, was one of the reasons he was attending my seminar.

I found several common symbols in Rajak's dream that are often in dreams among those converting from one religion to another. Needless to say, this is the most significant personal decision one will ever make; therefore, it elicits anxiety, which bubbles over into the subconscious mind's dreams.

There are dozens of well-documented dream cases where new or soon-to-be converted Christians have experienced wild and often frightening dreams. One theory behind this is that Satan is toying with the dreamer in an attempt to frighten him away from Jesus. I find that theory difficult to justify from a scriptural perspective because I find no biblical evidence that Satan has entry to, much less domain over, our dreams. Certainly Satan and his demon associates will mess with your mind and hit you at your weakest point, but I've found those tactics to be limited to waking and conscious thoughts. I believe dreams are the domain of God and His agents.

Trying to help Eric gain a better perspective, I began my analysis: "Rajak is sensing he is cutting himself off from his friends, his family, and his 'old self' in becoming a new creation in Christ. That's enough to cause anxiety and produce dreams in anyone, let alone a Muslim taking the big step.

"In any event, Eric, here's what the dream means to me. The significance of the dry riverbed is huge. Remember that it is the pathway he has walked for years, to and from Nepal. In essence, the pathway is his current religion, which he is now seeing as bone dry. In terms of dream symbols, a dry riverbed denotes death and despair, the polar opposite of a running river's meaning, which denotes life and personal prosperity.

"The fact that the riverbed starts to fill with water as he is walking *toward* you and your outreach ministry means his subconscious understands that both you and your message represent eternal life. Remember that the water is flowing *toward* you and *away* from his home. In other words, life—i.e., Jesus— flows like a river, but it cannot be attained at his home," I said.

Starting to grasp the significance of Rajak's dream, Eric stated, "When the river turned to blood in Rajak's dream, he became very frightened that it might be a symbol that he would be killed or die a violent death if he converted to Christianity. I told him I thought the river of blood meant the blood of Christ in the holy sacraments. What do you think?"

I commended him for his interpretation. "It likely does represent a river of life rather than a river of death. This is a vast departure from how secular psychology views a river of blood. In fact, one dream dictionary I recall says that rivers with blood represent trouble, gloom, and sickness. Quite a different picture from a Christian's perspective of salvation and eternal life in heaven, no?"

"Very different indeed," Eric agreed. "But what about the friends and family on the riverbank? I understand the part about their reaching out, trying to keep him from getting to Nepal, but why does he choose to remain in the river of blood? That's the part that has Rajak so disturbed."

I was curious about what Rajak had known about baptism previously and asked Eric about what he and the other missionaries preached. Eric explained that full-immersion water baptism was a concept that Rajak understood and had even witnessed. He went on to explain that baptisms were done at a local river, and that those baptized were leaned backward and completely submersed into the water.

"That's what I get out of his standing in the rising river of blood and then lying backward until he rests on his back at the bottom," I added. "In fact, evidence that he wasn't drowning comes when he said he lay on his back underwater for several minutes. The next image he saw was that of several large black fish circling above him. Eventually the fish saw him, at which time he needed to rise to the surface for air. This is where it gets a little sketchy, and without Rajak here to answer questions, I just have to surmise the meaning," I said with a note of caution.

Fish have many dream connotations. For the secularist, fish often represent birth and life issues, but for a Christian, they tend to symbolize one's current spiritual self. In other words, healthy fish represent a healthy spiritual life, and sickly or dying fish represent a spiritual struggle.

"Because Rajak's fish were large, black, and circling in a menacing way around him, my sense is that is how he views himself in his current spiritual state. Just a hunch, but I'm guessing large, menacing black fish symbolize that he was feeling attacked by his old spiritual self while his new self was being baptized underwater. That theory is made stronger by the fact that the fish don't let him surface and he drowns," I concluded.

Eric nodded slowly and asked for advice about what to tell Rajak.

"Please tell Rajak that his dream is not the foretelling of persecution or death at all, but likely the result of one of two possibilities. First, it may just be his mind's way of dealing with the stress of his decision. Or it may be seen as a wonderful confirmation from God that he is making the right move. Tell him that his dream symbol of baptism followed by laying down his life for Jesus places him in some very fine company," I said encouragingly. "My hunch is that you have preached out of Acts 21:13, and your friend Rajak has taken to heart Paul's message to his followers that he is ready to die for the name of the Lord Jesus."

"Ah, yes, Acts 21:13," Eric replied. "That's my favorite area of Scripture, and we've spent a great deal of time in the book of Acts."

EPILOGUE

About six weeks after the seminar I received an e-mail from Eric, who had returned to India. In his note Eric passed along regards from Rajak, who accepted that his dream was affirmation from God. Today Rajak is part of Eric's street witnessing team.

CASE NOTES:

The Sudden Infant Death Nightmare

NAME: Ruth
AGE: 27
OCCUPATION: Legal secretary
MARITAL STATUS: Married, with 1 child (age 6 months)

Ruth came to see me at the suggestion of her family physician, who was treating her for sleep deprivation and anxiety. Ruth had sought medical advice concerning the panic attacks she'd experienced for several weeks. She told her physician that the attacks began immediately after her daughter's near suffocation in her crib from SIDS (sudden infant death syndrome). Ruth's physician prescribed a sleep aid and antidepressants, saying they would help her. His prognosis and the prescribed pills did little to ease her anxiety, however. He also referred Ruth to me after he heard about her very unusual dreams.

When we spoke over the phone, Ruth told me she had discontinued taking the sleeping pills because of a fear she might not awaken if her daughter had another SIDS episode. She also noted that when she did sleep, she had vivid and highly disturbing nightmares following her daughter's near death experience. Subsequently the fear of SIDS plus her nightmares caused her to get up to check on her daughter constantly. Her lack of sleep was causing work-related problems, and she was in jeopardy of losing her job. Ruth had no personal or family history of depression, panic, or other psychological disorders.

When she showed up for her appointment, I immediately observed how stiff and uncomfortable she appeared. I said, "I know this is really scary for you—coming in to talk about your daughter's near death and the nightmares—

but I promise that I won't put pressure on you to talk if you're not ready. Deal?"

Without a hint of a smile, Ruth sat and looked down at her feet.

"Ruth," I asked, "if you're up to it, could you tell me what happened that night and also describe the dream?"

"I can," she replied, "but it didn't help when I told it to my doctor, so I don't really know why you think it should help."

I explained that I had studied dreams and felt I might be able to help her if we could work together at it. I also made it clear to her that she needed to be only as graphic with the dream as she was comfortable with, but that I could help her more easily if I knew more details of the dream.

She appeared resolved and told me her story then: "I put my daughter to bed at her usual time, eight P.M. I stayed up and read for a little while and then went to bed around eleven P.M. Then I had a dream. I dreamed that my family was living in a dollhouse. It was one of those large, realistic-looking kinds that has all the furniture and looks exactly like a miniature version of our current home, but there was no top to it. I could see my husband and me sleeping, and I could see the dog on the floor in the kitchen. Everything was just like it really is, except that I was seeing everything from outside and above my home. It was sort of like I was working the video camera, taking a home movie.

"Then I zoomed in on my daughter's room, expecting to find her in her crib. Instead, her room had turned into a funeral parlor, and her crib was a small wooden coffin on a track of rollers. Following the track, I saw that it led to a grandfather clock," she said, pausing.

"Anyway, the lid was off the coffin, and I could see my daughter inside. As the coffin approached the grandfather clock, I could see that the clock had struck midnight, and instead of a bird coming out, it was my husband's head on a spring. The next thing that happened was my husband's head looked up at me and he started crying."

Continuing, she said, "Then the grandfather clock's big glass doors opened up, and I saw that inside there was one of those ovens, whatever they're called, at funeral homes that are used to cremate bodies. I could see people inside, but I couldn't make any of them out. My daughter's coffin kept rolling along slowly until it passed through the opening. I could hear her crying for me right up to when the doors closed. Then I awakened."

I responded slowly, trying to comfort her somewhat. Coming from one parent to another, it was a pretty shocking visual. I asked her to tell me what she felt during and after she awakened from this nightmare.

Pausing to take a deep breath, she said, "During the dream, I had a creepy feeling that someone was controlling all the action, but I don't know who or why. When I awakened, I was really rattled by my dream so I went to check on Amber. When I looked down at her, she was lying on her tummy in her crib so I sort of watched her for a moment. You know how you look real close to see their little shoulders lift up and down while they're breathing?"

"I know exactly what you mean," I responded.

"Only she wasn't! She wasn't breathing! That's when I grabbed her and shook her and . . . nothing!" she exclaimed with tears forming in her eyes.

"And then what?" I prompted.

Clinging to a pillow, Ruth answered, "I just panicked and shook her by her shoulders really hard. At first nothing happened, but then she took this deep, gasping breath and started crying."

Even though I had already received the answer from her doctor, I asked, "And she was all right?"

"Yes, she came back! We rushed her to the emergency room, but the doctors thought I was just a hysterical female. They doubted that she had been without oxygen at all. They said she was probably sleeping soundly because all the tests came back normal," she said. "But I'm telling you, she wasn't breathing when I picked her up from her crib. I patted her while she was lying in her crib, and she didn't even stir. A mother knows how her baby sleeps and breathes, and I could tell something was definitely wrong. I knew she was either unconscious or dead."

"What did your husband say about it?" I asked.

"He believed me and still does. He didn't come in until he heard me screaming and the baby crying, but he knows I'm completely levelheaded. I'm a legal secretary. I don't panic," she stated firmly.

"My husband and his family are deeply religious Christians, and they keep telling me that God sent me this dream to keep my daughter alive. I was raised thinking God and angels and miracle stories are all sweet, but they are just around to offer hope to insecure people," Ruth commented.

I asked her to explain more fully and also to share what her husband thought about this.

"I think he's the one with faith and the one open to God. So if it was angels, then they should have their radar adjusted because they missed him by three feet and got me. And that just doesn't make sense to me," she contested.

Pausing for a moment, I stated, "Mind if I stick my two cents in here too?"

"Of course not!" she replied. "I know I came in defensive and standoffish, but I really do need to understand this nightmare so I can start to rest at night."

"Let's withhold judgment on whether or not this dream is of a divine nature for now," I said. "Your dream brings to mind one I studied in college. This case involved a nine-year-old boy who lived on a rural farm with his grandparents. The boy had been extremely sick with pneumonia and should have been in the hospital, but it was farm country, and getting to a hospital seemed out of the question.

"That night, his grandmother had a dream that her grandson was ice-skating on a frozen lake by their farm and fell through a crack in the ice. When she awakened from her nightmare, she rushed in to check on him and found him burning up with fever and in a coma. She knew nothing about nursing or emergency care, but somehow she got the idea to empty their freezer and pack all the ice around him. He was transported to the hospital in the next city, where the doctor told her that the boy's organs had all but shut down due to the fever. He said the boy probably had only a few minutes of life left had she not awakened when she did and thought to pack him in ice."

Ruth wanted to know if the grandmother thought it was a divine dream, and I told her I believed it was. The boy had grown up to be a pastor and led many people to Christ as a result. Had she not awakened that night and saved his life, he would have died.

"So you're telling me that you think my dream was from God and that He sent an angel to save her so that she could become a pastor? Is that what you're telling me?" she demanded.

"I don't know," I answered. "No one does, but I think your dream is consumed with symbols that point toward a spiritual intervention. If you'll indulge me for a moment, I think I can offer you some evidence," I promised.

"I'm sorry," Ruth apologized. "I snapped at you again. I don't know if it's the lack of sleep or the medication or my period, but I'm turning into a complete jerk," she said with a laugh. "You and my husband should form a support group."

"Forget about it," I said. "I doubt my insurance will cover it anyway."

Ruth laughed for a moment and then said, "Go ahead, I'm all ears."

Gathering my thoughts, I began, "The first symbol that strikes me is that you are looking down and seeing yourself, your family, and your home in a miniaturized version. Indulge me here, but if God is real, then this is the panoramic view He would have. Would you agree with that much?" I asked. I waited until I saw her nod her head yes before I continued.

"From there you look into your daughter's room, and you see that it turned into a funeral parlor. Your daughter's crib had become a wooden coffin, and it was on a track of rollers leading to a grandfather clock. A grandfather clock in dreams often denotes death in that it is associated with an older generation coupled with the expression 'time is running out,'" I commented.

"Several symbols were in play here. There was no mystery about the crib turning into a coffin. The fact that it was rolling toward the grandfather clock, which had just struck the midnight hour, was somewhat significant. Midnight shows up once in a while as a dream symbol and usually relates to zero hour or time being up, as I said earlier. But in this case, I believe that interpretation mixed with the idea that time is up.

"Ruth, an interesting symbol entered the mix next as your husband's head popped out of the clock instead of the usual bird. I can honestly say I've never heard that one before. It does, however, make sense in the context of your dream. Since your dream theme is *time is running out for your daughter,* and he looked at you and started crying, it appears that even though he was connected to time running out, he doesn't seem to be at all in charge of it. He actually comes across as helpless in your dream.

"Finally the grandfather clock's doors opened, and there was a crematorium inside. Your daughter's coffin moved through the doors and into the fire. You could hear her crying, and you awakened," I said. "That's the end of your dream, but then the real-life nightmare picked up as you went in to check on your daughter and found her lifeless."

I asked her if there was anything I had missed, but she said it was all there in front of me.

"Question," I began, "help me connect four key symbols because they don't make sense to me. They are, number one, time is running out; number two, your husband; number three, your daughter; and number four, your daughter's death. How do they go together?"

Ruth thought a moment, looked at me with a surprised expression, and said, "I think I know how they fit together. A couple of days before my dream my husband and I were having dinner with his parents. We got on the subject of baptism, and I told them that I hadn't made up my mind about baptizing Amber. Rick's parents are the nicest people in the world, but they acted as if I had just told them we were going to worship Satan in our home. Rick's dad went on and on about how children must be baptized at six months at the latest. He actually scolded me, saying that if Amber died, she could be in jeopardy of spending eternity in hell—away from everyone in the family, except me."

"Tough conversation," I observed. "How did it end?"

"It ended with me getting upset and telling Rick's parents to butt out. It was not their decision. We actually left, and there were definitely hard feelings on both sides," she recalled. "Rick and I argued about it all the way home and right up until bedtime. I've never seen him so upset about anything in our marriage."

"This is all starting to make sense," I observed. "The grandfather clock represents your father-in-law and his insistence that time is running out on the decision to baptize your daughter. Her crib turned into a coffin and slid through the grandfather clock into hell, which denotes his comment about putting her eternity at risk. Your husband's face appeared on the grandfather clock and relates to how your husband felt trapped in the middle of this argument, but ultimately took his father's side.

"Ruth, that poses a more difficult question for us now," I suggested. "It was actually easier when the nightmare made no sense. In that scenario, we could simply claim divine intervention, which caused you to check on your daughter. But now we see that the dream clearly fits the model of repressed anger and anxiety following a confrontation with your in-laws."

Ruth stared at me for a moment and then asked what her next step should be.

"Well, I'll tell you what I'd do if Amber were my daughter and I'd just gone through what you endured," I said. "I would err on the side of safety because complex coincidences bother me. This isn't some simple coincidence where you and your husband both bring milk home from the market. We're talking about your daughter's life. What are the odds that you'd have a death dream about your daughter at the precise moment she stopped breathing? Probably off the chart," I surmised. "No, this is definitely not a simple coincidence.

"What I'm trying to say is that I'd rather assume that God inspired me to check on my daughter because it wasn't His plan that she pass away. If I take this position, I have everything to gain and nothing to lose. On the other hand, if I default to the belief that my dream stemmed from hostile feelings and do not take action, then what happens if I'm wrong? What if I ignore God? What if God's message is to baptize her, or perhaps if not to baptize, to get my own spiritual life in order so that I can start raising my child with a belief system and let Him get on with His plan?" I stopped for Ruth's response.

"So you're saying I should let her go to church with my husband and in-laws?" Ruth asked.

"Ruth, you have to do whatever your conscience tells you. As for me, I choose to follow Jesus and heed the Scriptures where He warned, 'Do not put the Lord your God to the test' [Luke 4:12]."

EPILOGUE

I stayed in touch with Ruth for the next several weeks. Oddly enough, she did not have her recurring nightmare for almost four weeks. Then it returned one evening. She again checked on her daughter and found her sleeping normally.

The following day I spoke with her by phone. Playing a hunch, I asked her if in the previous twenty-four to forty-eight hours, she had dealt with church, baptism, or some spiritual issue. Not to my surprise, she stated that she had agreed to go to church with her husband, but later decided to go out to lunch with her mom instead. She didn't know if the dream recurrence was caused by guilt over backing out of her commitment or if it was a divine message. In any event, she said she would be attending church next Sunday even if just to be better safe than sorry.

Ruth's case points out two provocative dynamics about dreams and their origin. The first is that of God communicating to a nonbeliever through dreams. Clearly there is not enough space in this book to list the biblical references of how God speaks to the righteous and the unrighteous. Therefore, if He continually communicates to and pursues all of His children, in many ways dreams should simply fall into the list of His options.

The second dynamic Ruth's dream surfaces is that of discounting. Because of her spiritual distance from God, Ruth could clearly see an easier path in front of her if she discounted God's involvement in her dreams. After all, if it was God, then she'd have to examine her life and her current course of action with her child's religious upbringing. On the other hand, if she discounted the possibility of God's intervention, then she had to deal only with the conflict between her in-laws, her husband, and the baptism issue.

CASE NOTES:

Horses, Snakes, and Fathers

NAME: Julie
AGE: 25
OCCUPATION: Graduate student (psychology major in
                  doctorate program)
MARITAL STATUS: Single

Julie made an appointment to see me about a dream she first had when she was twelve years old, but she had experienced it off and on through the years. She characterized the dream as intriguing and mystifying, but also particularly disturbing. Her intention in bringing her recurring dream to me was simply to try to understand it.

Greeting Julie, I asked her if she felt comfortable enough to launch into talking with me about her dream. She agreed readily but admitted she was having more trouble than she thought she would understanding her dream, being that she was studying to be a psychologist.

Smiling, I answered, "Julie, it's not at all unusual that you are missing the interpretation of *your* dream. When Jesus said, 'Physician, heal yourself,' in Luke 4:23, I'm certain He wasn't referring to self-dream analysis. As you are learning, we've got so many defense issues surrounding and protecting our minds that it's very difficult to set them aside long enough to get a clear view of our own dreams."

"Spoken like a true Freudian analyst," she said, laughing.

"Actually, Julie," I said, "I'm about as far from a classical Freudian analyst as I could possibly be. Freud conducted his work through some rather secular and humanistic lenses, whereas I am utterly devoted to our spiritual connection with God as being the foundation of all things emotional."

"But what about when it comes to dreams?" Julie asked. "Don't you think Freud had it together? I mean, he was the father of analysis and dream interpretation, after all!"

"Actually no," I said, smiling. "I think Carl Jung had it more spiritually and psychologically together in his life and in his theories of dream analysis. Let's not minimize Freud's contributions, but psychology has elevated him to godlike status, and we've become so open-minded to his theories that our brains are in danger of spilling out."

With a slightly sarcastic but friendly tone, Julie replied, "Oh, I heard you were big into the Christian psychology thing. Well, I'll try not to hold that against you."

I noted her sarcasm and put on a benevolent smile, assuring her I appreciated her generosity in that regard. Then I encouraged her to tell me her dream.

"Sure," she replied. "Shall I start with when I first had the dream or with the latest version of it?"

"What would Dr. Freud say?" I asked, smiling.

"He'd say that it was all my mother's fault and that I must have had a bad experience with my oatmeal spoon when I was three," she mused.

"Touché!" I replied. "Why not start at the beginning? When did you first have this dream?"

Squinting at the ceiling as if the answer were hidden in its recesses, she explained that she was between eleven and twelve when she first had the dream. She believed it was the summer between those years.

I was pleased she was able to pin it down that specifically and asked her how she was able to get it down to only a three-month span of time when it was so many years ago.

"Well, I had the dream just after returning from a summer camp my parents sent me to," she replied.

"May I inquire into the type of camp you attended and your interesting choice of words about your parents sending you?" I asked.

"As soon as I said it, I thought you'd never let that one pass," she responded. "Well, the camp was a church-sponsored junior high camp in the mountains, and I didn't want to go. My parents went to church religiously—pun intended,

Doc—and thought it would be good for me to be away from my worldly juvenile delinquent friends for a couple of weeks. So, they packed me up and sent me kicking and screaming to God camp."

"I see. And you had this dream a short time after returning?" I asked.

She looked puzzled and admitted she had never put the two together before.

"If you don't mind, Julie . . ." I paused. "I've changed my mind and would like to hear your most recent version of your recurring dream."

"No problem. Okay, hold on to your seat. Here's the way it always happens," she said, drawing a deep breath. "In my dream, my dad and I were at this riding stable where they rent horses for the hour or day or whatever. My dad picked my horse for me and chose one that I didn't like from the get-go. I objected to this horse because it was way too big and it didn't seem to do what it was supposed to do. It was even hard for the stable guy to control. The stable guy was this little person, and he proceeded to try to talk my dad out of making me ride that horse. My dad and the stable guy got into an argument over it, but my dad won. I had to ride the mean horse."

"And what happened next?" I encouraged her.

"Well, I was just sitting there, crying and scared to death of this horse, and just about when I thought my dad was going to change his mind and not make me go riding, he got even angrier. See, I told you this was a crazy dream," she said after letting out an uncomfortable laugh.

Humoring her, I replied, "You sure did. So what happened next?"

Drawing another deep breath, she replied, "My dad was so ticked that he decided to teach me a lesson by taking the saddle off the horse and making me ride it bareback. Then he got on his horse and grabbed the lead rope from mine, and we started to ride into the countryside. My dad's horse was really tame while the whole time my horse was bucking and trying to scare me, but he wouldn't let me off."

"What do you mean, he wouldn't let you off?" I asked.

"I mean that each time I tried to get off the horse, he sped up so I couldn't without killing myself," she responded. "But by now, my dad was so angry with my attitude that he stopped my horse and told me to get off. Then he released my horse, which proceeded to follow me while my dad left me way out in the woods."

"And in your dream, what did you do next?" I asked.

"I just sat down on the ground and cried," Julie said. "I was terrified of being left all alone in the woods, but it got worse. At night I couldn't see a thing, but I could hear animals growling and following me around this dark forest. That's when I came to a huge tree that I thought would provide safety and sanctuary from the animals. So I climbed way up high into the tree, and as I was coming close to the top, I could see some sunlight peeking through the branches. I thought I was going to be okay until this green poisonous viper crawled out onto my branch. The snake kept slithering toward me, and I kept moving farther and farther out on the limb until it broke under my weight. Then I fell."

"And my guess is that you awakened prior to hitting the ground?" I asked.

"You got it right on the nose," she replied. "I just keep falling and I know I'm going to die, but I awaken before I hit the ground."

"While it's still fresh in your mind," I said, "describe your feelings and emotions for me."

"My emotions are easy to recall," she stated. "I experience a combination of extreme anger and extreme fear. An intriguing sidebar to my life after each time I have this dream is that I am ticked off at the world for the next few hours. It literally takes that long for me to snap out of it and put it back into perspective that it was just a dream."

"I understand how invasive these dreams can be in real life, and I commend you for being able to handle it as well as you have," I said.

I was forming a belief that she had a more developed spiritual side than she was letting on. Probing this area further, I asked, "You mentioned that the camp your parents sent you to was of a spiritual nature . . ."

"You mean God camp?" she interrupted.

"If by 'God camp' you mean it was a church camp, then yes," I replied.

Julie confirmed that it was, in fact, a church retreat in the mountains sponsored by the Catholic parish where her family used to attend church.

"I didn't realize you were raised attending church," I said. Sensing her response, I asked, "Are you still involved in church?"

Somewhat surprised at my question, Julie replied that it was just a phase her folks were going through when she was young. They stopped going to that church when she was about fifteen. Even though her parents started going to another church, they didn't make Julie or her sister go. Julie dropped out of church after that.

"And your sister?" I inquired. "Does she still go to church?"

"Oh, yeah. She's still all over the religious thing."

I asked her why she had chosen to stay away from church to this day.

"I don't mind you asking at all," she replied. "I just think religion, but especially church, blinds people to what's really happening in life. There's so much hypocrisy in the church. You know—do as I say, not as I do."

Nodding my head in agreement, I said, "Well, I'll give you that hypocrisy does exist in the church, although I'd assert that there will always be hypocrisy where people are called to a higher good because people will always fall short of the standard set by God." Sensing I was on the right path, I concluded, "The problem, Julie, is when people try to cover up their mistakes and hide behind religion."

As I watched for confirmation that I was on target concerning the connection between her recurring dreams and her problems with religion, my hunch was rewarded when her face flushed and her voice raised a decibel or two.

"You are so right!" was all Julie said to my point.

"Julie," I began, "let me see if we can take the mystery out of your recurring dream. I need to ask you up front about any counseling you've had since your twelfth birthday. I'm especially interested in any *issues*. Sorry, I hate that word, but I need to know of any counseling you may have received regarding physical or sexual molestation."

Julie stared at me for a moment, shaking her head slightly side to side while searching for a reply. "I'm speechless. How did you know that I had been in counseling for sexual molestation?"

I replied, "Actually I wasn't one hundred percent sure, but it was a calculated guess based on your dream coupled with the fact that you feel extreme fear and anger when you awaken from these dreams. Then all I had to do was factor in the way you react to spiritual issues, and it all started to paint a picture."

"Okay, Doc," she countered. "That was, as you say, a calculated guess. What do you think my dream means?"

"Here's what I make of your dream, Julie, starting with the prominent symbols. The first symbol you told me about was the little stable guy. The fact that you described him as little and that he got into an argument with your dad about forcing you to take the wrong horse is significant," I commented. "Julie, my assertion is that the little stable guy is probably you or your mother, but either way, that will surface in a moment.

"The second symbol we need to look at is the horse," I said. "Here's where you can rely on your old friend Freud to draw out the dream significance of horses. Horses often hold a sexual connotation in dreams. It's generally understood that horses take on this meaning to people because of their exposed genitalia and absolute lack of modesty in relieving themselves or mating. It's particularly noteworthy that your father was trying to teach you a lesson, so he removed the saddle and, in your words, made you ride the horse *bareback.*"

Summing up what we could presume to that point, I told Julie, "We basically know that you are led somewhere you do not want to go. You feel scared, unsafe and, most important, angry. Then someone small and relatively insignificant in your life, in comparison to your dad, tries to come to your aid by protecting you from a person who has some sexual connotation to you. Are you with me so far?"

"Yeah, I'm with you."

"Good, let's look at the other symbols and how they play into what we already know, shall we?" I asked without stopping for an answer. "You provide another symbol when you say that you want to get off the horse, but it keeps running and won't let you. In essence you're saying that you feel powerless against the horse and that it has power over you and that trying to get away from it, or making it stop, would only cause you pain."

Pressing on, I said, "Then your dad left you out in the wilderness with the horse that kept following you. What you're telling me is that you felt abandoned and alone in a strange place with a man who would not leave you alone, sexually speaking, that is. How are you doing?" I asked.

"I'm fine," she replied. "Please continue."

"Now we'll take a look at the part of your dream where you are lost in the forest and you come across a big tree. The interpretation of your climbing a big tree is that trees represent life and sanctuary—as in for small animals and birds—but of greater significance to a religious person, a chance to get closer to God and His safety. This is made even more likely by your description that you could see the sunlight, which represents freedom and safety, as you climbed upward.

"Next let's look at the final significant symbols, which are the limb of the tree and the poisonous snake," I said. "Climbing outward and away from the safety and security of the tree trunk tells us that you were going out on a limb by telling somebody something that you were very frightened of telling. By virtue of the poisonous snake crawling out after you on this limb, I would infer that means that someone dangerous was forcing you to tell something you were frightened of saying. Ultimately you told the truth, and the snake, or person, whom you told on, ended up winning in some way.

"Now, Julie," I said calmly, "let's tie it up in a nice package and see if it makes sense to you. In your dream you have told me that you went to a religious camp that you didn't want to go to. Your father wanted you to go and your mother supported you in not going, but your dad won out. At camp, you encountered someone whom you saw as powerful, or in charge, and this person either made you sexually nervous or physically touched you inappropriately. You tried to get away, probably by calling home, but your father wouldn't support your coming home. You felt that no matter where you went in this camp, this powerful person was there and in control over you. He was probably a camp counselor or an older boy who was attending the camp. Which was he?" I asked without missing a beat so as not to allow Julie a chance to obstruct her feeling.

"He was the camp counselor," she said in amazement.

"And when you got home, you told either your father or your mother, but no one believed you. In fact, because the snake—think of the serpent in the Garden of Eden—forced you to crawl out on the limb and ultimately to fall, my hunch is that the counselor and probably the people involved with the youth camp called you a liar. And if I'm not mistaken, that's the event that turned you away from God and religion," I concluded. "Can you give me an idea how you're feeling and how close I've come to connecting your dream to your real-life emotional injuries?" I asked.

"You are exactly on target," she replied. "It was a camp counselor who used to touch me inappropriately whenever he got a chance. Whether it was while we were all swimming or taking a hike, every time I turned around, it seemed that he was right there. I tried to tell my parents, but my dad wouldn't listen. He said I was probably being too sensitive. Then when I finally came home, I told my mom what happened, and she completely freaked out. She told my dad, and he wouldn't change his tune. He maintained that I was just a teenage girl and that I probably mistook the counselor's flirting and friendliness as inappropriate. When I wouldn't let it go, my dad met with the camp counselor. The counselor lied to my dad and said that I had been coming on to him and that I was making it up because he told me to back off."

Easing back in her chair, Julie said, "Look at me. Here it is thirteen years later, and I'm completely ticked off and shaking. I'm still so mad at my father for not believing me, my mother for not protecting me, and that pervert counselor for being a sexual predator and then lying to make me look like a crazy slut, I could just scream. I've had it! Whatever it is I need to do to be rid of this baggage I'm willing to do," she declared with resolve.

EPILOGUE

In subsequent sessions I learned that Julie, like so many other victims of physical and sexual abuse, had just let the matter go. We talked about how it is so difficult, if not seemingly impossible, to confront an abuser, especially one connected to the church, without the trust and support of your family. Even though it had been thirteen years, I encouraged Julie to follow a three-step plan.

The first step was to file a police report against the camp counselor. I cautioned her that because so many years had passed since the incident, the police might try to discourage her account. I also encouraged her to assert her rights and to insist that a report be taken. The reason was not to seek punishment for her abuser, but to bring this matter into public record, especially in the event that the counselor was still working with children today.

The second step was to contact the board of elders of the church that ran the camp. She needed to file a report with them so that they could take steps to ensure that this type of abuse was not going on today. I was clear with Julie that she was, at no time, to insist on or anticipate receiving an apology from the church. I told her to expect some form of risk management on their part, which she was not to take personally. It's not her fault that we live in a time of duck and cover and plausible deniability.

The final step was to write a letter to her parents informing them that she is contacting them out of love and not blame. She needs to tell her father, in particular, that she was indeed abused by the camp counselor and that he should have taken her word for it instead of siding with the counselor. Again, as with the previous letter, she was to expect no apology or anything remotely resembling acceptance of blame. That is not why I counseled her to enter this process. My rationale was that by confronting her abuser through the legal system and the authority of the church, she would no longer feel silenced and disbelieved. The letter to her parents was sent not to pick a fight but to unburden her secret, which housed her guilt and shame.

I met with Julie four weeks after she had accomplished each of these items. She reported her father still believed nothing had happened, although her mother privately apologized for not supporting her at the time. The police tried to persuade her that it was too late for her to file a report until she threatened to take the matter to the district attorney's office. And finally the church board of elders stated they would look into the matter, although she could tell that nothing was ever going to be done about it. The best news, however, was that she had not had her recurring nightmare since our meeting and she finally felt that she was no longer a victim.

CASE NOTES:

On-the-Air Dream Affair

NAME: Sandra
AGE: 33
OCCUPATION: Manager of a child care center
MARITAL STATUS: Married 6 years, with 2 children

Sandra called the radio station and told my producer she desperately needed to speak with me about a dream she'd been having for the past month. Having worked with producer Rob over the past two years, I could always tell by his expression when a particularly interesting dream call was on hold. Glancing down at my computer screen of waiting calls, I read: "Sandra, age thirty-three, nutcase or has a direct line to the Man upstairs!"

"Hello, Doctor," she said in a monotone voice. "My name is Sandra, I'm thirty-three years old, and I think my husband is having an affair."

"I'm sorry you're going through this. Can you tell me a little about why you suspect he's having an affair?"

"Sure," she replied. "I think God is speaking to me in my dreams. He is telling me that my husband is having an affair. I believe He's warning me, and I'm looking for confirmation."

I explained that I understood her point of view and asked for other signs that her husband was having an affair, but she responded that she had no evidence to give.

"When did you first dream that your husband was having an affair, Sandra?" I asked.

"God visited me in the first dream four weeks ago," she answered.

"Let me take a moment to clarify something if I may, Sandra," I said, pausing. "You say you have seen no evidence that your husband is having an affair, correct?"

"That's correct," she replied sharply.

"And have you confronted him with your dream suspicions?" I inquired.

"No," she replied impatiently. "Why would I reveal my one source of truth? He'd just think I was crazy, like your producer thinks. You know you should really tell Rob that he should make sure somebody's fully on hold before he starts making those *Twilight Zone* sounds. He's very rude."

Glancing up at Rob through the soundproof glass, I saw him roll his eyes and mouth the word *busted*.

"I apologize for Rob," I said. "He was absent the day they taught phone etiquette. But back to my question, why haven't you confronted your husband about your dream?"

"Because it's pointless. He's not a spiritual man, and he would never admit he was having an affair, even if I showed him pictures—let alone if I told him I saw it in a dream."

"Okay, Sandra, when did you have your first dream?" I asked.

"Like I said, I had my first dream four weeks ago on Monday the thirteenth . . ."

"Sorry to interrupt, but how is it that you recall the exact date of your dream?"

"Because I was at a two-day conference for child care providers, and the hotel where the conference was being held was a lot closer to my sister's home than mine. My sister had a couple of days off, so she asked if I wanted to stay with her and the kids during the conference," she replied.

"I'm with you now. Please continue."

Sandra began revealing her dream slowly: "In my dream I was present in my own home. I was walking around the living room and kitchen. The best way to describe it is that I was like a ghost. No one could see me or hear me. My husband was watching *The Ten Commandments* on TV in our living room. That alone is odd because he says the only things worse than movies about the Bible are chick flicks; he would never watch either! I walked around him a few times and actually stuck my hand in front of his face to make sure he couldn't see me."

"And could he?" I asked.

"No. He looked right through me at the TV. Next I walked down the hall to our kids' room, expecting to find my children sound asleep, but in their place were my sister's kids," she continued.

"Do you remember any emotions when you found out your kids were gone and your sister's kids were in their place?" I wondered.

"Not at all. It seemed perfectly normal," she answered. "Then in my dream, I walked back to the living room where my husband had changed his clothes and cut his hair. He was wearing dark blue pants and a dark blue shirt. He picked up the phone and started to dial my sister's phone number. I got scared that he was going to call my sister's house looking for me and that if I wasn't there, he would be really disappointed in me."

"Why do you think he'd be disappointed if you weren't there to take his call?" I questioned.

"I don't know. I guess because I'm trustworthy and I always do what I say I'm going to do," she commented. "Then I was back in my sister's home and picked up the phone, knowing it was my husband. He asked if I had been out of the house tonight, and I said I hadn't. Then he asked if I was going to come over to pick up my sister's kids or whether Pete would do that."

"Who's Pete?" I inquired.

"Pete is my sister's ex, and he comes to our house about once every two weeks to pick up his kids when it's his weekend," Sandra replied. "I told him that nobody was going to be by to pick up the kids. He said that was good because he'd been sound asleep and so had the kids. I didn't tell him that I had just seen him watching TV. I let it go because he was acting really guilty. I knew he was covering up something. Then I found out what it was. We have call waiting, and I heard his line click. He said he was putting me on hold to see who it was, but instead of being on hold, I could hear everything they were saying."

"Everything who was saying?" I asked.

"My husband and that harlot tramp who lives next door to us," she stammered.

"Slow down for a moment, Sandra. We're going to need a scorecard and jerseys to keep up with all the players in the game," I cautioned. "Shall we call her the harlot tramp, or does she have a name?"

"I'm not going to use her name because she may be listening to this program and then she'll know that I know," my caller admonished me. "But let me tell you what they were saying. My husband told her that I was out of town and that he just spoke to me on the phone and that it was safe for her to come over because the kids were asleep."

"And what did the harlot say?" I asked while catching a glimpse of producer Rob rolling around the control booth in laughter.

"She said that she'd be right over and that he'd recognize her because she'd be wearing *my* purple negligee. Can you believe the audacity! That he'd be cheating on me in my own home and that he'd give her *our* favorite negligee to wear?"

"You're right, Sandra. Purple is a hard color to look good in," I said. Producer Rob lost a mouthful of soda at that point.

I heard at least a tiny chuckle from Sandra before she replied, "Purple isn't a hard color for me to pull off, but that's not what I called you about. Then I just sort of popped over to my home again, and there I was in my living room. That's when I heard the doorbell ring. My husband bounded out of his chair like his feet were on fire. He opened the door, and sure enough, there she was. All two hundred pounds of trashy neighbor woman were stretching out my purple negligee."

Seldom have I ever lost it as I did at that precise moment. I dared not even glance at my producer if I ever wanted to regain enough composure to finish my program. Fortunately my studio microphone was equipped with what they call a sneeze button that allowed me to turn off my microphone before Sandra could hear the uproarious laughter that was now rendering ineffective what I thought was soundproof glass.

Fleeting childhood thoughts ranging from my dead hamster to Old Yeller finally enabled me to regain a modicum of professionalism before inquiring, "And what happened after your husband opened the door?"

"She marched in like she owned the place, looked right at me, and handed me a key chain with a key on it," she replied.

"I am almost afraid to ask," I said. "But did you recognize the keys as belonging to anyone, or could you tell what they went to?"

"Darn straight, I recognized the key chain. I've had it for over a year. It's got a little family portrait sealed in plastic on it. We had it taken in one of those little phone booth photo stops at Marine World Aquarium and Wild Animal Park," she replied.

"Fascinating," I said. "We're starting to run a bit short on time, Sandra, so could you wrap up your dream for me?" I said in a tone that sounded too much like begging.

"I'm sorry, Doctor," she responded. "Like I said, she handed me my key ring and walked right past me like she was snubbing me. My husband and the tramp started kissing, and I got so furious that I woke myself up."

"How are you feeling emotionally when you wake up?" I asked.

"I'm just as furious at him, or even more, as I was in my dream."

"Tell me something about your neighbor lady," I said.

"I cannot stand that woman!" Sandra snapped. "I get so sick and tired of her. She's divorced and she's always needing something fixed, and since my husband is a carpenter, she's constantly asking him to come over and look at this, or come over and look at that . . ."

"But other than the fact that you feel she imposes on your husband, do you have any suspicions about her intent?" I questioned.

"Well, you tell me, Doctor. What would your wife say if your divorced neighbor lady came over in skimpy outfits, batted her false eyelashes, and was all the time asking you to come over and take a look at this and that? Your wife wouldn't put up with it, and neither am I," she concluded.

"And is this dream the same each time you've had it?" I inquired.

"Essentially," she recalled.

"Let me work through some of your dream symbols because, unless I'm wrong, we need to establish three things. First, we need to know if it's likely that your dream is from God. Second, if it is from God, then what is He saying to you? And finally if it is *not* from God, then we need to understand what your dream is saying. I'd like to test a theory by asking you a few questions. Are you okay with that?" I asked.

"You're wasting your time that I made up my own dream. That dog won't hunt, but go ahead and ask away," she contended.

"Sandra, you said you first had the dream while you were staying with your sister. Correct?"

She acknowledged this fact and then told me a little more about her: "We're very close, and I've been really troubled for her over the last year. She's divorced from her husband and has been living alone for about two years. I keep her two kids in day care at my house, and she picks them up after she gets off work."

"In your dream, your husband suddenly appeared in a uniform. Do you know any men who wear uniforms?" I inquired.

"No one that I can think of," she replied slowly. "My husband is a carpenter, and my dad is a salesman, but other than . . . oh, wait, my brother is a butcher at the Super T market. He wears a uniform."

"Dark blue pants and dark blue shirt?" I questioned.

"No, he wears a white butcher apron and a white shirt with a bow tie," she replied.

"I think it's safe to rule out your brother. What kind of work does your sister's ex do for a living?" I asked.

"He's a fireman," she hesitated. "Oh, I guess I forgot about him."

I asked if she had seen the ex-husband during her visit with her sister. She explained that she had. He had come to her house to pick up his children after his graveyard shift on Friday. He was still wearing his uniform when she saw him.

"Let's go ahead and dive in and see what we can make of these dream symbols," I said while glancing at my notes. "You describe yourself as a ghost in that you are walking around your house and that no one can see you or hear you. Ghosts are unique dream symbols and can mean a variety of things to a variety of people, but because you described it as if no one could see you or hear you, it takes on a heightened significance. My suspicion is that we're dealing with a part of your life where you feel unnoticed, unappreciated, unloved, and so on."

"That's a little bit on the *duh* side, isn't it? I mean, if God visited you in a dream and told you that your wife was having an affair, wouldn't you kind of feel like you were unloved? That was very insightful," she mused.

"Try to keep an open mind while we're peeling back the layers of your dream, okay?" I asked, but didn't wait for a response. "Then your husband was watching *The Ten Commandments* on TV in the living room. Is there anything out of the ordinary in this scene, other than that you said your husband doesn't like Bible stories?"

"No, but that's unusual enough for a dozen dreams right there," she replied.

"A prominent symbol comes into play in this scene in the biblical connotation behind *The Ten Commandments*. Because of the direction the rest of your dream takes, we can feel safe in construing this symbol to be about sin . . ."

"You're darn tootin' it's about sin. How many thou shalt nots do you figure he's breaking here? Thou shalt not commit adultery and thou shalt not covet thy neighbor's wife. Now that I picture her in my purple negligee, I'm thinking he's also busted on the thou shalt not covet thy neighbor's ox commandment," she announced triumphantly.

"Lest we get into casting first stones at those who may or may not be without sin, we should just continue," I advised. "I said the dream is about sin, but I didn't say it was necessarily your husband's."

Continuing, I added, "The next thing you did in your dream was to walk around him a few times and place your hand in front of his face to make sure he didn't see you. Close your eyes and think of this part of your dream, and then tell me which hand you were placing in front of his face."

A moment passed before Sandra replied, "I had my right hand on the back of his chair, and I was waving my left hand in front of his face."

"That's significant in that you are waving the hand that bears your wedding ring in front of his face. And why are you waving your hand in front of his face?" I asked without providing a break for an answer, "because you are trying to get him to notice you. Therefore, this symbol potentially speaks of your feeling lonely, unnoticed, and unloved, and you are trying to remind your husband, and possibly yourself, that you are married.

"The next part of your dream features you walking into your kids' room, expecting to find them asleep, but in their place were your sister's kids. This symbol forces us to stretch because we aren't just talking about you and your husband any longer. Now you've introduced four other people to your dream. Your sister, her kids, and her ex. Are you still with me?" I asked.

"You're not telling me anything I haven't told you so, yeah, I'm with you," she answered.

"You then walked back to the living room, and your husband was in a dark blue uniform and he had cut his hair. We eliminated everybody in your world, including your brother the butcher, so we know that the only blue uniform in the family belongs to your ex-brother-in-law. So if you're collecting the evidence, you have to notice that your brother-in-law has shown up twice now.

The first time through the connection with the kids and then in a uniform that appeared on your husband. Let me take this scene apart one more layer by asking you what you think it means that your husband had a haircut?" I asked.

"I don't know. Maybe he just needed a haircut. Why? What does it mean?" she posed.

"Hair has a few meanings, but the most accepted have to do with virility and sexual performance. So, by virtue of the fact that he had a fresh haircut in your dream, I would have to ask you if your husband has recently experienced any sexual dysfunction or if there has been any distance in your sex life."

"That's a coincidence," she granted me. "He is a diabetic, and when his blood sugar gets out of whack, he has trouble in bed. His doctor has been trying to get him to try that drug that works wonders for men, but he isn't interested in taking anything."

"That's helpful to know because that explains some of the previous symbols. To recap: you are invisible to your husband, you're waving your wedding ring in front of him to remind him you are married, and there's been sexual frustration in your marriage. These symbols fit together. The symbol that sticks out like a sore thumb is that of your ex-brother-in-law."

"But what does all that have to do with my husband calling me to make sure I wasn't coming home and then inviting the neighbor over for two minutes of bliss, if you know what I mean?" she interjected.

"Let's dig a little deeper into your dream symbols to see if they help. In your dream you noticed that your husband was calling you at your sister's home, so you magically appeared in time to answer his call. This is symbolic of how you are feeling emotionally distant from your husband, but also that you still want to be there the moment he calls. You said you didn't want to disappoint him by not being there. This could mean that you don't know when intimacy (aka the call) may return to your marriage, but when it does, you're afraid you won't be available to him emotionally. Let's just tuck this away for now to see if it is relevant to later symbols.

"In your next dream sequence your husband seems to be testing the water to see whether you are coming home to pick up the kids or whether it will be your brother-in-law," I said.

"That's ex-brother-in-law," Sandra corrected.

"Yes, that's ex," I conceded. "In any event the dialogue then followed along a route that introduced your ex-brother-in-law again. That time he might come over to pick up the kids. In that same sequence, your husband lied to you about being asleep, even though you had been watching him while he was watching TV. Someone sleeping in your dream can denote that you feel that something about that person needs to be activated or brought to life. It's pretty clear that we're talking about your husband's sexual problems that you wish were activated or aroused.

"We're nearing the solution to all this, so let me know if you get lost anywhere, Sandra," I said. "The next thing that happened was your neighbor appeared at the door wearing what you refer to as *our* favorite negligee—check that—*our* favorite purple negligee. I need to ask you a question and I want you to know I'm asking this for purely scientific reasons, but what is special about your purple negligee?"

"I'm not going to say anything except that it was the negligee my husband bought for me on our honeymoon," she replied. "And before you ask, yes, I do still have it, but no, I haven't worn it in years. And I know you're going to ask why, so let me just strike first in saying it doesn't fit me anymore. There! Are you satisfied?"

"I understand, and I'm sensitive to what you're saying," I assured her. "The fact that your negligee dream symbol shows up on the neighbor starts to make a lot more sense. Is it safe to infer from your comment that all two hundred pounds of her stretching out your negligee equates to her being a large-framed woman?"

"Well, yes, she's large, but I'm probably just as large as she is," Sandra said almost dejectedly.

"Hang in there, Sandra," I consoled. "If you'd like, I can give you the number of a weight-loss support group in your area. Let's finish this dream matter, and then you can let me know."

I reflected on the fact that the next stage of the dream involved the neighbor woman handing Sandra the key chain with a key attached as she marched into Sandra's home and started kissing her husband. Keys are important dream symbols; they represent the desire to release what has been locked away or out of reach. Keys can mean opportunities to explore an unconscious feeling or an impulse. I felt there was a good chance that I had a reasonable theory for her dream.

"You're going to tell me that this dream isn't from God, aren't you?" Sandra demanded sharply.

"The interpreter is not the one who should make that determination, Sandra. The dreamer is. But I will tell you that your dream symbols all point to your dream being a normal, human release of pent-up anxiety."

"But what about his watching *The Ten Commandments* on television and the connection between that and his cheating on me? Doesn't that strike you as a message from God?" she demanded.

"Actually no," I replied. "It seems a bit tacky that God would reveal something this significant through a Charlton Heston movie. I think it makes more sense that you directed and starred in your own dream movie. Let me start, and you can stop me at any time that it starts to feel uncomfortable, okay?"

"Go for it. I mean, it's not like anyone else can hear what I dreamed and know that I'm a fat woman who sees her neighbor lady walking around in her purple negligee," she said sarcastically while laughing nervously.

"That's the beauty of radio," I encouraged her. "You're anonymous. Besides, everyone has his own problems to worry about, and yours aren't all that glamorous. Let me tell you what I think we've got going on in your dream. We've established that the headliners in your movie are you, your husband, your ex-brother-in-law, and your neighbor. I'll give away the surprise ending up front by telling you that you are playing a dual role. You play yourself in most of the movie, but then you also appear as the neighbor woman."

"Oh, my gosh, are you kidding me?" she exclaimed. "I'm that tramp?"

"No, I'm not kidding you, and no, you are not a tramp," I assured her. "Every symbol in your dream points to an intimacy crisis in your marriage. This crisis has taken on a sexual connotation in your dream, but that's just the symptom. The problem is intimacy. You revealed it in your dream when your husband showed up with a haircut. You revealed it again when you saw yourself as the neighbor woman wearing your intimate wear. Interesting how symbols work like that, isn't it? And you provided the key symbol in the final act when *you*, playing the neighbor woman, handed a key attached to your key ring to *you*. This was the key to unlock the intimacy in your marriage."

"You haven't explained my ex-brother-in-law. How does he fit in?" Sandra asked in a perplexing tone.

"Your ex-brother-in-law is a transference symbol. That's when we take the image from one person and transfer it to another in our dream. My theory about your ex-brother-in-law's significance in your dream is first and foremost, he's divorced from your sister. That means that he represents your unconscious fear of what may happen to you if you don't solve your intimacy crisis. I think his image also brings out other possibilities to your dream. For instance, it may be that you . . ."

Stopping me cold, Sandra stated, "Hold it right there. That's about as far as I'm comfortable in going."

"Fair enough," I replied. "Let's not go there. I do, however, want you to consider that your poor self-image has left its fingerprints all over your dream. You may see yourself as unattractive at the same time your husband sees himself as impotent. One or both of you are going to have to break the silence and deal with this intimacy problem."

Glancing at producer Rob, who was pointing to the clock, I said, "Sandra, thanks for the fantastic dream and for being so willing to enrich the audience by sharing it. If you'd like to hang on, I'll put you on hold and have my producer give you a couple of referrals for you and your husband in your area."

"Thanks, Doctor Greg," she replied. "But tell producer Rob to go easy this time."

EPILOGUE

Approximately four weeks later, I received a surprising off-air phone call from Sandra telling me that she took my suggestion and started a weight-loss program. She tried to get her husband to go to a marriage counselor with her, but to that point, he had refused. She also informed me that she and her counselor were satisfied that her husband was not having an affair and that her dream was more likely a result of her marriage struggles. Sandra took great delight in pointing out that I was wrong and that her dream had nothing whatsoever to do with any repressed sexual feelings she may have had for her ex-brother-in-law.

CASE NOTES:

A Dearly Departed Dream

NAME: Toni
AGE: 23
OCCUPATION: Teacher
MARITAL STATUS: Married 2 years, with no children

Toni made an appointment to visit me, stating that she needed to explore a dream she had just experienced. She referred to the dream as "the most wonderful dream of her life."

Don't think for a moment that therapists rank their patients according to some ideal scale, but if we did, Toni would have scored high marks. She arrived ten minutes ahead of schedule, was tuned in to her feelings, and communicated well, but most of all, Toni kept a dream diary complete with significant thoughts and emotions she had experienced following her dreams. The only way she could have scored higher would have been if she had shown up with a tray of homemade cookies for extra credit.

Upon taking her seat, Toni wasted no time in getting down to business: "I had a dream about my mom who passed away about two years ago. I spoke with my pastor about it, and he told me that even though he didn't know much about dreams, he thought it wasn't very likely that my mom visited me in my dream.

"Then I visited the priest from the church where my mom used to attend, and he said he thought it was totally possible that she visited me. He said I should light prayer candles for her spirit and pray for her to come to me again in my dreams. What do you think?"

I smiled and told her I was impressed at how quickly she had seized on the whole thing. She was eager to get through the mixed messages received and clarify the issue.

Starting immediately, she said, "I had the dream for the first time about a month ago. We, that is, my whole family and me, were at the lake where we used to go every summer on vacation. We had great vacations and family reunions at that lake.

"Anyway," she continued, "in my dream, my dad and my two younger brothers and I were in our family's boat. We were cruising around the lake in slow motion—sort of sitting around killing time with no place to go. When my mom was alive, we all water-skied or fished or just messed around, having fun. But in my dream, nobody was talking or having fun. My dad wasn't teasing my brothers like usual, and we were all just sitting around staring at each other."

In anticipation I asked, "And that's when it happened?"

"If you mean if that's when my mom entered the dream, then yes," she replied.

I prompted her to continue.

"I was driving the boat, and we came to this narrow passageway that leads through the mountain. We had never seen it before, and we were about to turn around when my mom appeared on the bench seat at the back of the boat," Toni said, smiling. "She was just sitting there with sort of an odd expression on her face. It was kind of like when she was frustrated with one of us, but too sweet to get mad. She just frowned a little and then gave us a half smile to let us know she wasn't mad."

"And what happened next?" I inquired.

"She looked at me and pointed her finger toward the passageway leading through the mountain. I looked at my dad and brothers, but they didn't say anything. I looked back at my mom, and she just motioned straight ahead toward the opening and then looked back at me and nodded her head and smiled. I steered the boat toward the opening, but the water inside was really choppy and looked dangerous. I looked back at my mom to see if she really wanted me to enter that opening. She gave me a calm smile and nodded her head like she was reassuring me to go through the opening. Then she faded out of view.

"I steered the boat into the passageway, and it started to rock pretty violently. I was starting to get nervous that we wouldn't make it. Then I noticed that there was another calm lake on the other side of the passageway. My dream ended before I knew if we had ever made it through to the other side," she concluded.

"Can you pinpoint any feelings inside your dream and immediately following?" I probed.

"During my dream, I felt pretty edgy and nervous, but when Mom appeared, I just felt calm and happy. While I was steering the boat through that passageway in the choppy water, I felt pretty scared. But when I awakened from my dream, I was left with this sense of being overwhelmed. It's sort of like I used to feel in college when I had a ton of studying to do and little time to do it."

Collecting her thoughts for a moment, Toni asked, "My parents' priest told me that the happy feeling I get when my mom appears in the boat is confirmation that she did come to me for real and I'm not just dreaming it. Tell me, what do you think?"

"Toni, I'd like nothing more than to tell you that your mom visited you in a dream because I know what kind of joy and comfort it would bring you," I said. "I try to judge all tough spiritual issues through a prism of 1 John 4:1–3, which directs us to 'test the spirits' to determine what is truly of God and what is not. In this case, we have to see what the Bible says about those who have passed away and are now in heaven, and about whether they are able to contact us through dreams or any other means."

Scripture reveals that God used dreams and visions more than two hundred times to make personal contact or to send a message via an angel of the Lord. Only the book of Acts documents two instances where Paul was contacted by a human vision—that is, an earthbound being other than God or an angel (Acts 9:12; 16:9). In both cases, however, God was present and directing the visions.

Looking at Toni, I said gently, "Unless God directed your mother into your dream for a purpose as significant as those we find in the book of Acts, we have no biblical precedent for thinking that's what happened with your mom."

"Then if it wasn't my mom visiting me through my dream, was it just nonsense?" she asked with frustration.

"A great question," I told her. "As I said, it's unlikely that God changed the rules and allowed your mom to *physically* contact you in your dream, but in no way was your dream nonsense. In fact, it was significant, if not monumental, in importance. I think God created our minds in such a way to allow us to reach into the memory to access people we've lost. The apostle Paul frequently wrote about *remembering* those who are no longer with you. In Philemon 4 he wrote, 'I always thank my God as I remember you in my prayers.' In a very real way—physically, emotionally, and intellectually—your memory allowed you to visit your mom in your dream.

"*She* didn't access *you*, but *you* were able to access *her* through an indelible imprint of your mom in your mind. She's an irrevocable part of you. Your mom influenced your very essence. That means that depending on circumstances in your life, you're likely to retrieve images of your mom via your dreams. Think of it as a consultation to help you work through a tough situation."

"So you're saying the mom who visited me in my dream was the memory of Mom that is always present in my heart and mind?"

"That's clearly correct," I answered. "Look at it in one of two ways: either God broke the pattern and chose to allow your mom to access you through your dream, or God built you in such a way that encourages you to access your mom through your memory. Either way is evidence of God's genius. Now the key for us is to figure out what's been going on in your life that prompted you to seek your mom's guidance through your dream."

"I don't know," she said. "Can you point me in the right direction?"

"Absolutely," I replied. "Let's see if your dream symbols hold the answer. First you told me that you were with your family on the boat at the lake where you used to go on family vacations. Let's take the dream symbol of the lake first. A lake in a dream generally denotes life. From there, a lake that is choppy represents an unsettled life while a smooth lake represents a peaceful life. In your case, the lake you are on appears peaceful enough, but you are headed into a bit of choppy water.

"It's also important to note that your family was on a boat when your mom appeared. Boats mean a lot of things in dreams, but they usually represent an object used in transition—to get you from one emotional place to another. For instance, a boat stuck on a sandbar would mean something different from a boat speeding along on the open lake. In this case, however, your boat was moving in slow motion toward a narrow passage in the side of the mountain," I said.

"I'm confused about the boat thing," Toni interjected.

"Okay. Let me go at it a different way," I replied. "If you were struggling with problems at work, a boat in your dream could be the vehicle or the way you would go about switching jobs. Say you're a mom and your fifth grader is failing school. If you dreamed of you and your child on a boat, we'd be talking about how the boat represents the *way* you will find your child the help he needs. Does that help?"

"Yeah, that helps a lot," she said while nodding her head.

"You helped me even further in how you described the experience on the boat. You used an interesting term when you said your family was just 'killing time.' You said that nobody was talking and you were all just sitting around staring at each other. To me, killing time on the boat reveals that the transitional period you and your family are in following your mom's passing feels lifeless, distant, and lacking in direction. Do you see how all these symbols are starting to tie together?" I questioned.

Responding by leaning forward in her seat, Toni replied, "I get it now. So it takes on even more significance that my mom appeared in the back of the boat while we are in transition, right?"

"Bravo! That's the next symbol. The back of the boat isn't your mom's usual place on board. Now she's taken a *backseat* to whom?" I asked.

"To me?" she questioned.

"Precisely," I affirmed. "And she's directing you toward a narrow passage featuring choppy water between two calm lakes. This is a prime example of what we call a *problem to solution* dream symbol. In other words, the lake you and your family are currently navigating in your dream feels distant and lifeless without Mom. Then she appears and points you toward a narrow opening, which isn't exactly smooth sailing, but the other side looks beautiful. The passage through the opening is the rocky journey that promises to be a challenge, but will lead to a happier life," I commented. "How are we doing so far?"

"So far I'm with you one hundred percent," she replied, smiling.

Pushing on, I said, "Let's not miss what this dream may ultimately be trying to tell us. I think it connects back to the fact that you're driving the boat. Your being in the driver's seat says two possible things to me that I need your help with. Either your mom used to physically drive the boat on these outings, and/or she was the one who orchestrated family trips and took care of all the details. Which one feels more correct?" I asked.

"It's both. Dad used to sit in back with the boys, and they'd either fish or water-ski while Mom and I took turns driving the boat. She loved to drive that boat. You're absolutely right as well in that Mom was the one who took care of all the details. From packing to unpacking, Mom was the conductor," she said with a chuckle.

"That ties in nicely. So tell me what you make of driving the boat while Mom took a backseat and pointed out the direction?" I asked.

"I suppose that with Mom gone, I'm the one who's in charge, but she was helping by providing me directions," she said boldly.

"*Yes!* And driving the boat is a metaphor for what?"

"It's a metaphor for the journey my family and I are on," she replied.

"I think you're on target," I said. "And your next dream symbol confirms exactly that. Your mom was smiling, but sort of giving you *that look* as she lovingly pointed to you. What does that mean to you?"

After she thought for a moment, Toni's eyes lit up as she said, "She was passing the baton to me and wants me to fill in for her in planning what we used to call our *together family time*. That was really important to Mom. I also think she was saying that we've grieved and isolated ourselves long enough and avoided family vacations. She's saying that we need to go through the choppy water to get to the smooth sailing on the other side."

"You are a great student, and I think you've nailed your dream's hidden message," I replied. "Now let's see if this dream was triggered by an external event in your life or simply thoughts and feelings you may have been having lately. Any obvious connections between family, vacations, feeling distant, wanting to connect, and Mom?" I asked.

Placing her hand over her mouth indicating her surprise, Toni revealed, "It's so funny how this all ties together. A couple of nights ago, my husband and I were talking about getting Dad out of the house. It's been two years and he's gotten better, but he's still so down. He just doesn't seem to want to do things anymore. My husband suggested a family reunion at the lake, but I told him that it might be too soon and I just didn't know if I could deal with the emotions of getting everyone together at the lake."

"I concur. That sounds like the triggering thought that produced the emotions that filtered through in your dream," I affirmed. "It sounds like your conscious mind made a decision that your subconscious wasn't so sure was the right call."

"So, what should I do?" she inquired.

"Why don't you pray about it and talk with your husband, dad, and brothers? See what they think about a family reunion at the lake. If all signals point to having a reunion, then enlist their assistance in putting it together. If you do decide to have a family vacation, go into it with the understanding that it *will* be different. Emotions will run high for everyone, so it's best to talk among yourselves before you go and frequently during the vacation. If indeed you have accepted the baton you think your mom has passed to you to keep the family connected, then accept it without pressure or guilt. I'm certain your mom would not want you to fill in for her if it meant stressing you out or trying to measure up to her way of doing things. Just lock in on a mental image of Mom smiling and supporting your efforts."

EPILOGUE

Toni's dream is a great example of one reason the New Age movement has so much appeal to those who have lost loved ones. Because it's free to say things that don't wash with Scripture, this movement would claim that her mom absolutely spoke to her in her dream. It's a commonly held New Age belief that the spirit world has a direct channel to the living. New Agers believe that communication between the living and the dead happens all the time and is enhanced through the use of psychics and spiritual mediums.

I understand the appeal of their way of thinking. With as much unfinished business as we have following the loss of a loved one, it is wonderfully comforting to think he or she could pop in for a visit. The only problem with this philosophy is that it doesn't jibe with Scripture.

Instead, people of faith should recognize that we come factory-equipped from God with the ability to connect with people we've lost. Here are the conduits through which we connect:

1. Our prayers to God for and about our loved ones and through asking Him to pass along our love and thoughts.

2. Our conscious memories of a loved one.

3. Our subconscious memories and thoughts about loved ones, which surface in our dreams.

CASE NOTES:

Stalked by the Sting Monster

NAME: Tammy
AGE: 23
OCCUPATION: Dental assistant
MARITAL STATUS: Single

I had just finished a dream seminar at a church when a young woman approached me and stood off to the side patiently waiting for others to finish talking with me. As the last person left, she approached and said, "Hi, my name is Tammy. Do you have time for one more? My boyfriend insisted that I tell you my recurring nightmare."

With a sheepish grin she added, "This is the most bizarre dream with the strangest combinations of events, people, and places, and it's making us both crazy. None of us, not my parents or my friends, can figure out what it means."

"No pressure there. Now I'm being pitted against friends and family. How many lifelines do I get?" I joked. "You were in the class, so you know that I'll ask you a few questions and then we'll get into your dream."

"Fair enough," she agreed.

"Let's start with the basics," I said. "Do you remember what the three foundational questions are concerning recurring nightmares?"

Rolling her eyes upward in search of the answer, she replied, "Let's see . . . when did the nightmares start, how often do I have them, and . . . and . . . what type of feeling or mood does my nightmare put me in while I'm having it and after I wake up?"

"You took good notes," I complimented her. "So on to the three questions."

"I first had the dream about three years ago," she began. "And I have it about twice a year, maybe more, but when I have it, it completely ruins the rest of my night's sleep and bothers me for a couple of days."

I inquired what she had been doing three years previously, but she stated that there was little out of the ordinary, not even stresses, relationship problems, or deaths in the family. I asked her if she was trying to be challenging, but she assured me that there was little of excitement to lead into meaning in the dream. All that had happened was that she was in college, she assured me.

"And what feelings or emotions accompany this recurring nightmare?" I asked.

"It scares the snot out of me," she replied. "My boyfriend is so tired of hearing me complain about it that he told me to figure out what this dream means or I'm history! Well, he was kidding about that part, but we both just want to understand the dream so it will stop."

"I'm not sure it 'scares the snot out of me' is the correct clinical term," I chided, "but let's jump into your recurring nightmare anyway. Start at the beginning and tell me as much as you can recall in as vivid detail as possible."

"My dream takes place in England," she began. "I don't know why I'm in England, but I just am. I was in this huge gymnasium with an Olympic-size swimming pool in the middle and bleachers all around. I was standing on one end of the floor, but I realized that I had to get to the door at the other end of the gym." She added, "That was where it really started to get crazy."

"I'll be the judge of that," I said, smiling. "Please continue."

"Well, I couldn't get to the other door because inside the pool was the Loch Ness monster," she said with hesitation. "You know, the water serpent that shows up from time to time in Europe. Sort of their version of our Big Foot."

I assured her I knew what the Loch Ness monster was and prompted her to continue, assuring her that however crazy it got, I was listening attentively.

"It gets crazier from here," she cautioned. "Inside the pool was water, but the pool was also filled with exercise equipment, like in a gym. You know . . . weight machines, treadmills, and barbells. And this huge Loch Ness monster was swimming back and forth in the pool and stepping on all the gym equipment and watching my every move."

"You're not on any medication, are you?" I jokingly asked.

Tammy laughed and replied, "Not yet, but you may want to prescribe some when you hear this next part."

"You mean it gets weirder?" I asked.

"Yeah, I'm afraid so," she added. "This is where Sting comes in."

"You mean Sting as in the English rock singer Sting?" I asked, impressing myself that someone so out of touch with the world of rock music would recog-nize the name. "Dare I even ask what Mr. Sting was doing in your dream?"

"He was riding the Loch Ness monster like a horse," she replied.

"So, let me get this straight up to this point. In your nightmare, you were in England, and you found yourself in a gymnasium with a huge swimming pool. You were standing at one end of the gym, and somehow you knew that you needed to get to the other end of the gym if you were to get out," I summed up. "Is your impression that you are needing to escape the gym, but the only way out is the door at the far end?" I asked.

"That's precisely it," she replied. "Only Sting and the Loch Ness monster won't let me by. Every time I tried to run past them, the old Loch stuck his ugly head out of the pool and tried to eat me. I'm joking with you about it now, Doc . . . but in my nightmare, I don't know what's scarier, the monster or the musician. Both of them are creepy buggers."

"Creepy buggers," I replied. "Duly noted. Please continue."

"I just kept trying to get past them. First I'd try one side of the pool, and they would cut me off. Then I would run frantically around to the other side of the pool, and they would swim over and almost get me there too," she exclaimed. "Finally I was exhausted, and I stopped for a moment to catch my breath. And that's when I noticed them."

"Noticed who?" I asked.

"Noticed the people in the bleachers around the pool. They were full of people just watching me trying to get out of that place. Nobody was helping, and they didn't seem to be afraid for their own lives. They were watching like a bunch of zombies. I hate zombies, and I hate that they just stare at me like zombies," she concluded.

"Okay," I interjected, "I need to catch up, so check me on the details, right?"

"Shoot," Tammy said.

Drawing a deep breath, I said, "You were in England, stuck in a gymnasium with the Loch Ness monster, which was swimming in a giant swimming pool and being ridden by the rock star Sting. The only way out was at the other end of the gym, but each time you bolted for the door, Loch and Sting cut you off and tried to eat you. Last, you noticed the bleachers were full of people who were just watching you like zombies, and you hate zombies."

"Perfect," she said. "Now make it go away!"

"Let's not get ahead of ourselves," I cautioned. "I need one more piece of information."

"How it ends?" she asked sheepishly.

"Exactly," I replied. "Does your dream always end the same way, and if so, how?"

Pausing for a moment, Tammy replied, "Always the same way. I finally got so scared, angry, and frustrated that nobody from the stands would come to my aid that I decided to make a break for it. I decided to run for the door at the far end of the pool. At first, it looked like I might make it to the door, but the monster and Sting got to it just ahead of me."

"And?" I inquired.

"And they ate me!" she replied. "Why do you think they call them nightmares? Because I got out, and we all visited the queen of England and had tea and crumpets?"

"I didn't realize you were also a standup comedian," I said. "So your dream always ends the same way, with your being consumed, correct?"

"Always the same way," Tammy confirmed.

"I know I'm going to hate myself for asking, but can you distinguish which one, that is, is it the Loch Ness monster, Sting, or the two of them who actually do the consuming?" I inquired.

"I really can't tell," she replied, easing my anxiety only to increase it again. "I think it was a World Wrestling Federation tag-team sort of thing."

"Entertaining as this has been, let's see if we can't solve the riddle of this nightmare," I said. "Let's take a look at the prominent dream symbols one by one. The first is England, followed by the swimming pool, the gym, the exercise equipment in the pool, zombies in the bleachers, can't reach the exit, trapped inside the gym, and finally the tag team of the Loch Ness monster and Sting, who eat you. Did I miss anything?" I asked.

"Did I tell you the part about the president's dog?" she asked while maintaining a straight face as long as she could.

"Humorous. I'm assuming you've been to England?" I asked.

"Yes," she replied. "I was in England and Scotland while in college."

"About three years ago I would presume?"

"Yes, as a matter of fact, it was about three years ago," she affirmed.

"And since that was about the same time your nightmares started to occur, we need to look at events that took place while you were in Europe," I said.

Moving down the trail that logically made the most sense, I asked, "Did you meet someone in England and have a relationship?"

"No, I was dating my current boyfriend, who was back in the United States. I didn't really even go out with friends much while I was there. It was a university-sponsored study course so I was pretty busy," she explained.

Continuing to try to find a thread of logic between her real life and her nightmares, I asked, "Since there was exercise equipment in the pool, did you work out while in England?"

"No. I really hate exercise," she replied.

"Okay, no exercise," I said slowly while checking down my mental list of possibilities. "Somebody scared you while you were traveling in Europe. Did you meet someone who worked out or exercised around you? Perhaps you encountered someone while swimming in a swimming pool?" I asked.

"No."

Dreams are sometimes like a crossword puzzle in that when you get hung up on a clue, it's often helpful to work a connected symbol or two. Sometimes just getting a small piece of the connecting symbol jars the memory loose and reveals volumes.

"Let's move on to your next dream symbol, which would be the pool," I suggested. "Since you said you didn't swim at your hotel or exercise, my suspicion is the pool denotes the ocean. More specifically we could assert the ocean to be the vast ocean between England and the U.S. Therefore, we can deduce that the water means that even though there is a huge distance between you and danger, it isn't enough to keep you safe. So we can assume that your mind is trying to work through the fact that danger is waiting for you when you try to get back home or at home."

"I'm with you so far," she said.

Continuing rapidly, I said, "Give me three adjectives that pop into your mind when you think of the Loch Ness monster."

Thinking for a moment, she replied, "I think of *scary, elusive,* and *powerful.*"

"And when you think of Sting, the entertainer, what does his image conjure up for you?" I inquired.

"I guess he's a bit freaky. He's got some scary, psychotic-looking eyes," Tammy responded.

"We're on the right track now," I encouraged her. "So we're dealing with someone whom you viewed as scary, elusive, and powerful. This person likely had some freaky-looking evil and psychotic eyes that scared you. Ring any bells?" I asked.

"Not a single one," she said.

"Let's move deeper into your dream symbols then," I said. "The exercise equipment inside the pool is a tough one. My sense about it is that this scary person was very intimidating and overpowering in your eyes. A good place to start would be a large guy who worked out and was perhaps heavily muscled."

I continued, "The next symbol about being unable to escape the gym is somewhat easier. You simply felt stalked or trapped by this large, overpowering, psychotic-looking character."

Suddenly the direction of Tammy's dream became clear. "Tammy, who stalked or harassed you, either physically or emotionally, while you were in England?"

"I never put it together until you said it! It was that marine dude from my college who was on the trip. I didn't know him and neither did any of my friends, but he liked me in a scary way. He started hanging around us and would sort of conveniently show up everywhere I went. I finally had to tell him that I was engaged, but he didn't seem to care.

"You know what," she posed, although no question followed, "he was a workout fanatic. He was one of those marine commandos, Rambo-like, a muscle dude with those really deep-set, spooky eyes that freaked me out. *Just like Sting!* Oh, and I first ran into him when our class was in Scotland. This guy was around me throughout the rest of the trip right up to the time I left England for home. Is that why the Loch Ness monster showed up in my dream? Because that myth is Scottish, and this wacko first showed up in Scotland?"

"I think you are absolutely on target with that assessment," I said. "And by virtue of there being bleachers filled with staring zombies all around the pool, I'm guessing none of your friends would help or counsel you on how to get rid of this guy."

"You got it!" she exclaimed. "Everyone was just glad that Rambo was my problem and not theirs. And it freaked us all out that he was actually from our university and that we'd probably have to deal with him when we got back to school. And the being eaten by the Loch Ness monster and Sting part? What does that mean?"

"Being eaten in a dream simply translates into your fear that this guy was so omnipresent and all-consuming—lock in on the word *all-consuming*—that you were afraid for your safety. Hence, in your dream, you were eaten or consumed," I concluded.

Now that we had finished analyzing her dream, she wanted to know what was next. I explained that it should be less fearful now. Most likely each time she had experienced the nightmare, she probably would find a triggering event. Her most recent dream could have been prompted by a commercial on TV for the marines, a friend who was traveling to England, or even a Rambo movie on TV. Any of these events could have triggered an undiscovered or misunderstood dream.

"Did you have any contact with Rambo after you returned from England?" I asked.

"Not really. I ran into him a couple of times, but I ignored him. He must have moved on to another victim because I didn't see him after that," she concluded.

"Then my sense is that since you now know what the dream is about, you won't have the same reaction whenever you see or hear something that triggers that memory," I surmised.

Epilogue

Tammy's recurring dream was a classic example of how bizarre and seemingly irrelevant dream symbols creep into the feature film being shown in the theater of your mind. To Tammy, hers was a sick series in a dream that plagued her, and would continue to do so, until she finally mastered its meaning. Since I never spoke with Tammy after this interpretation, I never had an opportunity to ask her if her recurring dreams had ceased—although 90 percent of the time, this is the case. I also didn't have the chance to ask her what the president's dog was doing in her dream. Perhaps it was for the best.

CASE NOTES:

Death Prophecy

NAME: Jen
AGE: 23
OCCUPATION: Children's ministry director, homemaker
MARITAL STATUS: Married 1 year, no children

When I was actively doing my daily Christian radio program, I would dedicate one day a week to exploring dreams. On that day, to say that the phone lines would burn up would be an understatement. Toward the end of a particularly busy show, I received a call from a woman who identified herself as Jen, a twenty-three-year-old children's ministry director at her church. Jen presented herself in a very articulate fashion and seemed emotionally together.

Because of the sensitive nature of dreams, it was my habit never to ask a caller what church she attended, but it was always interesting to learn of the denomination or description, whenever possible. Jen stated she worked at and attended the same church. She described it as a large, somewhat conservative Christian church that does not preach or talk about the gifts of the Holy Spirit, such as speaking in and interpreting the gift of tongues (Acts 10:46; 19:6).

Jen's first question was broad and concerned the study of dreams. She asked how she should deal with three vivid dreams she'd had when someone she knew died. Because there was not enough time remaining in the program to do justice to both her question and her dream, I told Jen I would speak to her off the air. As common as dreams are where someone known to the dreamer dies, I had a sense this was going to be an interesting case.

After signing off from my program, I picked up the phone and greeted my caller: "This is Greg. Are you still there, Jen?"

"Yes, Doctor," she replied. "Please tell me you'll take the time to listen to my dream," she pleaded. "I've been to my pastor, and he told me that he didn't even want to hear my dream and that dreams can be demonic."

I took the next few minutes to walk Jen through many of the scriptural references to dreaming throughout the Bible. Concluding, I said, "Jen, I'm not here to debate the biblical foundation of dreams against your pastor. I can only tell you that I've been studying this subject for years, first from the perspective of a neutral social scientist and later as a born-again Christian. There is no margin of doubt in my mind that dreams belonged to God long before the New Agers moved in. Once that happened, dreams became tainted with the beliefs that they belong right alongside tarot cards and astrological charts.

"People who doubt the validity of scriptural evidence for divine dreams should look up scriptural references to dreams and visions in a computer concordance. Depending on the Bible translation, there are more than two hundred. Those in doubt should go through each one and read the circumstances surrounding the dream or vision and count the number that are connected to God and/or angels. If that doesn't convince them, ask them to look up Ouija boards, psychics, astrologers, tea-leaf readers, and palm readers in the Bible. If they find these individuals in the Bible and they have God's blessing, they have the wrong Bible.

"Just to finish this, Jen, if your pastor did research the Bible, he would find one reference to the formal title *astrologer* in Scripture," I said. "Interestingly enough, it's connected to the story of Daniel and his interpretation of King Nebuchadnezzar's dreams [Dan. 2:10]. Basically the story speaks to what a fraud astrologers were then. And one more thing: many, if not most, of the kings chronicled in the Old Testament routinely consulted with these types of so-called magi, or advisors, who oftentimes had their fingers in demonic, worldly, and unholy matters that were abhorrent to God," I concluded.

"Sorry if that seemed like a lecture, Jen," I added. "But it frustrates me sometimes to keep fighting to reclaim a biblical topic that has been a key in the shaping of Christianity as we know it. For goodness' sake, Jesus' very own birth announcement was delivered to Joseph in a dream [Matt. 1:20]. Sorry again, Jen," I said. "Now I'm really finished with the lecture."

"You don't owe me an apology, Doctor," she said. "I agree with what you're saying, and that's the reason I called you about my dream."

"I majored in preaching to the choir in college," I joked. "Please tell me about your dream."

"About three weeks ago, I had a dream that someone died," she said. "Then I had a similar dream about that person dying about five nights ago, and then again last night. At first I just passed it off as a weird nightmare, but I've been starting to wonder if it could be a God thing and if I'm supposed to do something about it."

"It's a little unusual to have three similar dreams during the span of about three weeks, but I'll give you my opinion on their possible origin after I hear the dreams. Before you tell me about them, tell me something about the person who died in your dreams," I said.

"It's my pastor," she said calmly.

"Say again?" I asked.

"It's my pastor," she repeated. "He's the pastor I was telling you about in the beginning. Remember, the one who doesn't believe in dreams and thinks they're demonic?"

Well, my instincts were right about this call, I thought. "So you had gone to your pastor to ask him his opinion of dreams in preparation of telling him about the three you had about his death?" I asked.

"Yes. We never got past the part where he didn't want to hear anything about my or anyone else's dreams. Now I'm afraid that if I don't warn him about the dreams, he really might be sick and not know it until it's too late," she replied.

"I see your predicament," I said. "Have you ever experienced premonitions before in dreams?"

"No, never before . . . in a dream," she stated.

Wondering why she hesitated, I asked, "Does that mean that you've experienced premonitions while awake?"

"Well, sort of a premonition, I guess," she responded. "About five years ago some friends and I . . . keep in mind I was a teenager . . . used to go down to the beach, and we'd visit a psychic. We'd go about once a week, and we'd take turns letting her tell us our futures. I was sort of into worldly things back then, and I didn't see any harm in it."

Continuing, she said, "Anyway, this one time, the psychic told me that she knew I was different from my friends. She said she recognized that I had some psychic powers, too, and that I should be trained in how to use them."

"And did you?" I asked, already sensing the answer.

"Well . . . yeah . . . I kind of did," she replied. "I visited her about six times, and she taught me something about being a psychic. Mostly things like looking at people's auras to figure out what's going on with them and stuff that I later found out was completely New Age. But I didn't know it at the time, and it was exciting."

"I'm not here to pass judgment on you, Jen," I said. "I know that the world is appealing, especially to young people, but tell me about the premonition you believe you had."

"I bumped into a girlfriend's mom at the mall one day, and while I was talking with her, I got this overwhelming feeling that something bad was going to happen to her," she said. "I wasn't even thinking about her aura or anything psychic at the time. It just hit me. I fully saw a vision of her in a hospital bed hooked up to tubes and wires. She could tell there was something going on in my head, and she asked if I was okay. I just told her I had a headache, said good-bye, and went away. I know she thought I was smoking dope or something.

"Then about a week later, I ran into my friend—the one whose mom I met at the mall. She told me that her mom was in a bad car accident. Apparently a truck had run a red light and broadsided her, and she'd been in the hospital for a few days. She was going to be okay, but she was really lucky to be alive. I turned white as a ghost and muttered something to my friend, and I think she walked away thinking I was on drugs too."

"I see. So you believe you had a premonition of this woman's traffic accident before it occurred," I said.

"Yes," she said. "Is that possible?"

"I think everything is possible to God, including visions, or what we call premonitions. The Bible documents more than a hundred cases where visions of the future are delivered by God or an agent of God," I answered. "So, if indeed you had a premonition, the question is, Who provided it to you?"

"Couldn't I have accessed some sort of psychic energy I had on my own?" she asked.

"It's a valid question and one I don't have an absolute answer for," I replied. "But whenever I don't have an answer to a spiritual question, I have to turn to the Bible. Interestingly enough, Jen, the Bible is not silent on this issue. There is a scriptural position, which indicates man alone does not have the capability to see visions or have premonitions. Evidence is found in Ecclesiastes 8:7, which states, 'Since no man knows the future, who can tell him what is to come?' It seems clear to me that people who have the ability to see the future, whether it's for a moment or a lifetime, owe that ability to one of two sources—either God or Satan."

Sounding confused, Jen questioned whether Satan had such power. She had been taught that only God can work visions and dreams.

"Remember the theme of 1 John 4, which instructs us to 'test the spirits to see whether they are from God.' Believers are being admonished for a reason, and I believe the reason is that Satan and his followers, both demonic and human, will try to lead us astray wherever they find a foothold. I think fortune-tellers, psychics, and the rest of their kind who dabble in the occult are fully involved in Satan's realm, whether wittingly or unwittingly," I said.

"But you really didn't answer my question. Can you tell me where it says that Satan has the power to control visions and the telling of the future?" she asked impatiently.

"Sorry, Jen, let me be more specific by citing Acts 16:16, where the author related the story of the fortune-teller by writing: 'Once when we were going to the place of prayer, we were met by a slave girl who had a spirit by which she predicted the future. She earned a great deal of money for her owners by fortune-telling.' We start to learn more about the slave girl in verse 17, which reads: 'This girl followed Paul and the rest of us, shouting, "These men are servants of the Most High God, who are telling you the way to be saved."' Finally we get the picture of *which* spirit is driving this girl in verse 18 when we read: 'She kept this up for many days. Finally Paul became so troubled that he turned around and said to the spirit, "In the name of Jesus Christ I command you to come out of her!" At that moment the spirit left her.'

"Jen, this scripture doesn't tell us how often Satan may have an influence over providing visions. We can infer that it is rare, especially when compared to the biblical references to God providing dreams and visions. It does, however, verify what I said about witting and unwitting pawns of Satan," I commented.

"Remember, this girl was a spirit-possessed fortune-teller who blended in as a follower of Christ until Paul saw through her disguise and called out her spirit. I'm not saying you were Satan's pawn when you were experimenting with fortune-telling, but you were headed down a dangerous trail that could have culminated in exactly that."

"I understand your point," she said. "Then how do we explain that I saw my friend's mom in the hospital?"

"I'd be lying if I told you that I knew for sure," I replied. "Perhaps God was trying to use you in some way, or maybe He used the vision to draw you closer to Him. That doesn't mean God has given you the gift of prophecy. It just means He may have been working with or through you for some greater good.

"Another possibility is that it had nothing whatsoever to do with God. In this case your vision came from one or a combination of circumstances such as psychological transference, déjà vu, dumb luck, or a psychic gift. I can understand all except the latter, which I cannot endorse either scientifically or spiritually."

"I know what déjà vu, dumb luck, and a psychic gift are, but what is psychological transference?" she asked.

"That's when you look at someone and for no conscious reason you think about someone else or a situation comes to mind," I answered. "If you could track the thought process, you'd find that your mind sees something that reminded it of something it had seen before. Next, it makes the connection and draws up that memory file. For example, let's say your friend's mom bore a strong resemblance to a woman you saw in a movie last year. In the movie the woman was involved in a horrible car accident and ended up in the hospital. Even though your conscious couldn't recall the movie to save your life, your subconscious has logged it, categorized every component, and stored it for future access—"

Interrupting, she said, "Then when I saw my friend's mom, my memory recalled the movie, and I misunderstood and thought it was a future event instead of a past memory, right?"

"Right," I replied.

"Wrong!" she insisted. "It was no movie. I don't care what you say."

Remaining calm, I turned to the task at hand. "I'm certainly no one to argue with God, and I don't wish to argue with you. If you think it was from God, then I'm fine with that. Let's say we tackle your recurring dreams about your pastor to see where they are coming from," I said.

"Let's, but before I do, you clarify the three possible origins of visions and premonitions again."

"As far as I can judge, based on theology first and psychology second, the first origin is from God. The second possibility is that you created a foothold for Satan to toy with you when you dabbled in the occult," I answered slowly so as not to be misunderstood. "Remember, Satan looks for weaknesses and invitations, and your dealing with the psychic was like sending out an engraved invitation for Satan to throw a party in your head. But please hear me when I say that even if he did have his hooks into you at that time, he could not exist in your heart now. Satan and God cannot coexist in the heart of a believer. And the third scientific possibility, and I underscore the word *possibility*, is that some people may in fact possess some *sixth sense* that gives them a heightened degree of sensitivity. Since science has documented so many cases of this, it would be imprudent to completely discount it. On the other hand, I have not studied it to the degree I have studied dreams, therefore I am only comfortable with the God-inspired or Satan-influenced scenarios. Okay? So the foundation is set. Now let's hear your dream."

"Well, like I said, I've had three dreams about my senior pastor over the past three weeks. In my dreams, I've got this sort of overhead view of everything . . . like I'm lying upside down with my back against the ceiling, but nobody can see me. Each dream started out with me watching my pastor in his living room. I could see him sitting in a big blue leather recliner, and the television was on, but nobody was watching it.

"Diane, that's his wife's name, was doing something in the kitchen, but I couldn't tell what it was. She looked up at this old grandfather clock on the opposite side of the room from the TV, and I could see that it was ten-thirty P.M. That's when she told him that she was tired and that she was going to go upstairs to bed. My pastor kissed her good night and said that he needed to stay up for a while to prepare for a funeral service. She asked him when he was delivering the service, and he said he didn't know, but it would be soon," she said.

"Then Diane started up the stairs. I could tell she was crying, but she was so quiet, my pastor didn't hear her. Next, he walked into his home office, which is on the opposite side of the house from the kitchen, and sat down at his desk. He removed a file from his top right desk drawer and opened it. Right away I could see that the top page of the file had a picture of my pastor on it. As he wrote, he said each word out loud, and I could tell that he was writing his own epitaph. After a few minutes, he closed his file and put it away. He turned off a yellow desk lamp and started up the stairs to go to bed. Halfway up the stairs, he clutched his heart, slumped to the stairs, and died."

"Fascinating dream," I commented. "Can you tell me what emotions you felt during and after this dream?"

"It wasn't as disturbing to me as you might think. I had a very peaceful feeling about my pastor, but I cried a little over the image of his wife as she walked upstairs crying. I don't know what that image means, but it was upsetting," she concluded.

"Understandably," I agreed. "We'll take a look at these symbols in a moment, but first, can you tell me about your second dream?"

"They were reruns," she replied. "Except for maybe a couple of small details that I couldn't even recall, they were the same. They were reruns. Doesn't that prove conclusively that my dream could truly be a window into my pastor's future?" she asked.

"Not necessarily," I replied. "It's possible that your mind just kept feeding back the same basic dream because of your frustration over not being able to talk with your pastor about it. In a way, it's like retaking a test that you need to pass before you move on to the next section. Your subconscious will keep repeating the dream until it feels that you got the desired result—in this case, your pastor's attention.

"Let's continue with the dream symbols so I can get a better grasp of how to direct you about your dream," I added. "A good place to start is your overhead view of the dream, coupled with the sense that neither your pastor nor his wife could see you. It's not unusual to dream of being invisible, which often denotes a feeling of insignificance, but the noteworthy symbol here is your description that you had your back to the ceiling. This is what I call a *perspective symbol;* these symbols are generally more important in analyzing a dream than many of the other symbols. You see, dreaming that we are invisible is fairly common in a dream, but having the *perspective* of your back to the ceiling and looking down at your dream are significant.

"You have the overhead perspective that God might enjoy," I continued. "Except, and this is important, you are positioned between God and your pastor. This translates into your belief that you may have God's point of view regarding your pastor, but you also have physical access to him.

"Now take a look at your second symbol where he's in the living room. The living room is no mystery at all. Your dream started in the *living* room because that is the present condition of your pastor—*living*," I explained. "I can't make heads or tails of the big blue leather recliner, though. Perhaps you own such a recliner or the pastor has one in his office?" I inquired.

"No," she replied hesitantly as if to think of all the chairs she has seen in her world. "I don't recall seeing such a chair anywhere except in my dream."

"Then let's move on to the next symbol, which was the television," I proceeded. "TVs in dreams are usually incidental to a secondary symbol, which is either what is on the TV or, in this case, the fact that it was on, but nobody was watching it. Turn this symbol into the phrase 'no one is paying attention to it,' and what do you feel, Jen?" I asked.

"That no one is paying attention to me," she replied. "You mean that I'm the TV?"

"Not at all," I replied. "But you are identifying with the TV in that you're providing noise, but no one's paying attention. The TV is a metaphor for how you are feeling. Does that make sense to you?" I asked.

"Actually, Doc, it does. Thanks."

"Your next few images are very informative in this dream," I continued. "You told me about an old grandfather clock. Clocks in dreams nearly always mean that the dreamer feels she is up against a deadline and that time is running out. I'm curious, however, that you see an old grandfather clock. Does the pastor have a grandfather clock in his church office, or do you own one?" I asked.

"No, I've only seen a desk clock in his office, and I only wish I had a grandfather clock," she replied.

"Then we'll simply settle on the logical conclusion. How old is your pastor?" I inquired.

"I'm not sure, but I'd guess in his mid-sixties," she said.

"Then because of his grandfatherly age, we'll make the short connection that the clock represents your pastor and is foretelling that time is running out for him," I suggested. "I've been thinking about the next symbol, which is the time on the grandfather clock—ten-thirty P.M. Does this time of the evening mean anything in particular in your world?" I asked.

"Not really," she replied. "My husband and I are night owls, and we usually don't go to bed until eleven-thirty or twelve—sometime after the news or later."

"All right then. We'll put that into the incomplete pile and move forward," I continued. "Next the pastor's wife said she was going to bed and started upstairs. He kissed her good night, which is probably just a projection on your part that they have a warm relationship. It probably wasn't germane to the dream. But the next part sure was. That was where he said he was staying up for a while to prepare for a funeral service. Preparing for a funeral service could also mean preparing for *what?*" I asked.

"Preparing to . . . die?" she replied.

"Precisely," I agreed. "But the key phrase is what follows when, in your dream, you observed his wife ask when he was delivering the service. Pay close attention to the fact that she didn't ask *who* had died, but instead focused on *when* the service was. That tells us that there was no doubt *who* was dying, only *when* he was going to die. Your next image was of her walking upstairs crying, yet her crying was so faint that the pastor couldn't hear her. In this image, you've likely taken on the emotions of your pastor's wife. You are separating from your pastor both physically and emotionally. You're doing so physically in the metaphor of walking up stairs while he is left behind and emotionally in that you are crying out to him, but he isn't paying attention to you.

"So what we know so far is that your dream symbols are coming together in a theme, which is: *nobody is listening to you, time is closing in on your pastor, he's preparing to die,* and *you are beginning to separate yourself from him.* With me so far?" I asked.

"Everything you've interpreted is true," she replied. "It's exactly how I'm feeling."

"The next scene took place in the office in his home," I continued. "You saw him at his desk, and he removed a file from his top-right desk drawer and opened it. I'm not sure what to make of the specific location in his desk where he removed the file. Does that particular drawer mean anything to you?"

Closing her eyes to focus, she replied, "I can't think of anything significant about the top right-hand desk drawer."

"Not a problem. We'll set that image aside with our big blue leather recliner and move on to the file itself. Files in a dream denote important documents, usually of the legal variety. In your dream he removed the important documents, and by virtue of his picture being on the top, the theme is confirmed that this is all about him," I said. "If someone else's picture had been in the folder, we would have had to move in a different direction, but we're confident now that it was legally documented that he was the focus of your dream.

"Your next symbol confirmed all the other symbols and theme," I said resolutely. "He was writing his own epitaph. Therefore in your dream, he was preparing to die. And finally your dream concluded with him turning off a yellow desk lamp, which I'm going to lump in with our mystery objects, and starting up the stairs. You saw him get halfway up the stairs before he clutched his heart and died. It may, or may not, be significant that he was halfway up the stairs when he died. It could denote that there is a between heaven and earth connection, or that he was too young to die, or that he had unfinished business, but it may not matter what it meant exactly. Likewise, I'm not sure clutching his heart had any greater significance than his denoting his death.

"It seems fairly conclusive to me that your dreams were about one of two things. The first possibility is that they reveal the anxiety you feel about the potential loss of someone you are close to. Perhaps you think he doesn't take care of himself as far as health and diet are concerned. By the way, does he?" I asked.

"Not at all," she replied. "And I'm on him all the time about it, but I don't think that's it, so what's the other possibility about my dreams?"

"The other possibility is that God is intervening somehow and communicating something through you," I responded. "Now we have to determine which is which. I think I know a way.

"Your dream occurred in considerable detail in that you described a blue leather recliner, a grandfather clock on the opposite side of the room from the TV, an office located at the other side of the house from the kitchen, and a desk with a yellow lamp. I think we can solve this by asking the question: How many times have you been in your pastor's home, and if so, have you been in each of these rooms you described?" I asked.

"With God as my witness, Doctor, I've never been in my pastor's home!

I've never even heard anyone describe it or seen pictures. I couldn't tell you if it's one story or two."

"I believe you, Jen, so here's what I want you to do. Since your pastor doesn't really seem eager to talk to you about dreams, I want you to take a different route. I want you to call the pastor's wife and ask her about the blue chair, the grandfather clock, the yellow lamp, and some of the items that you dreamed in detail. You don't necessarily have to tell her it was a dream. The important part is to find out if the images are actual or fictitious dream symbols. Can you do that and then call me back with her response?" I asked.

"Of course," she replied. "Only I don't know if she's at home or wherever. I'll see if I can track her down and then I'll call you back." Jen thanked me and hung up the phone.

EPILOGUE

According to my chart, three days passed before I received a voice message to return Jen's call. Since so much time had elapsed, I had concluded that she had abandoned her pursuit or had learned from the pastor's wife that none of those described items existed in real life.

When I returned Jen's call, she told me she had spoken with the pastor's wife, Diane, concerning her dreams. They agreed to meet at a coffee shop where Jen found Diane to be much more receptive to the possibilities surrounding dreams than her husband was.

Jen told me that the pastor's wife listened intently to her entire dream account. Except for the fact that Diane began to tap her finger nervously as Jen described the room decor, the pastor's wife revealed nothing.

When she concluded her dream, Jen said she felt like a complete fool and fully expected to receive a lecture from Diane. Instead, Diane confirmed that they live in a two-story home with a grandfather clock, a gift from her parents, which sits in the family room opposite the TV. Jen stated she instantly allowed her mind to accept that a grandfather clock is a fairly common item and many people would place one in the family room. Therefore, this really didn't prove anything. It wasn't until the pastor's wife described the pastor's favorite blue leather recliner that both realized this dream was no fluke. Jen went on to say that everything, decor wise, matched up between her dream and their actual home, except for the yellow desk lamp on the pastor's desk. That symbol remained a mystery.

The pastor's wife also confirmed that she had been worried about her husband's health for several months. In fact, she had tried to get him to go to the doctor for a physical several weeks prior, but he stubbornly said he had no time.

Jen concluded our conversation by thanking me for sorting out her warning dream. She said there was no doubt in her mind that Diane took the dreams seriously and that she was going to insist that the pastor have a complete physical, even if she had to drag him there herself.

I did not hear from Jen after that phone call. The scientist in me always looks for irrefutable proof in unusual and potentially divinely inspired dream scenarios, but sometimes that is impossible. In these situations, I have to rely on my instincts about people. So the question becomes, Do I believe Jen and conclude that she had received a divine warning dream, or do I think she was imagining this or, worse, lying? Based on ten years as a cop and ten more in private practice, I'm satisfied that she was telling the truth.

CASE NOTES:

Crucified in Your Dreams

NAME: Dennis
AGE: 19
OCCUPATION: Student
MARITAL STATUS: Single

I received a phone call from a pastor friend asking for a favor. He asked if I would visit with a young man from his church who had just returned from a six-month mission trip to Korea. My friend told me only that since this young man's return, he had been having a tough time sleeping.

Having had experience working with Christian missionaries, I was aware they sometimes endure difficult readjustment periods upon returning to the States. For whatever reason, my friend didn't tell me that Dennis's sleep issues were related to some very disturbing and recurring nightmares.

"So Pastor Rick tells me you've been back in the States for about a month," I said, easing into the conversation.

"Yes, sir," he politely replied. "I traveled with a group of missionaries from our denomination to North Korea about six months ago. Some of my team members are still there, but I decided it was time to come home."

"So is it nice to be home again?" I asked. "And by the way, call me Greg."

"Yes, sir . . . uh, Greg, it's nice to be back," he replied. "Except for . . ." He trailed off.

"Except for what?" I inquired.

"Except for the nightmares I've been having," he said. "That's why Pastor Rick suggested I come see you. He's concerned about my nightmares."

"Yes, Pastor Rick did mention you'd been having some trouble sleeping, but he didn't comment about nightmares. Perhaps I can help you figure them out if you'd care to share them with me," I said.

He replied that it couldn't hurt.

I thanked him for the huge vote of confidence but was privately glad he had at last cracked a smile. Then I launched into the session by asking if he had experienced the nightmares more than once.

"Yes, sir. I've had the cross dream about once every ten days or so for the last two months," he replied. "I've had some other doozies, but the cross dream is the one that breaks me out in a cold sweat. It's so real."

I asked him if he meant "cross" in the religious sense, as in the symbol. He quoted John 19:17 to me, explaining that he meant the cross on which Jesus was nailed at Golgotha. I encouraged him to tell me his dreams.

"Okay, here goes," he began. "But I warn you, you may want to get me fitted for a straitjacket after you hear this. In my dream I was hiking along the outer ridge of Paektu-san on the Korea-China border. Paektu-san is actually a dormant volcano, and it's also the highest peak in North Korea. Anyway, I was hiking it alone at about fifteen thousand feet when I came across a small group of American missionaries. I recognized some of them, but others were strangers.

"I don't know why, but in my dream they made me uncomfortable," Dennis continued. "Then I recognized one of the guys. He was the missions leader from my church back home, and he told me they were waiting for me because there was a family emergency and I had to go home. They refused to tell me what the emergency was, but I somehow knew that it was my grandfather. I could see his image in my dream. He was lying in a hospital bed back in the U.S. and had suffered a massive heart attack.

"I panicked because I didn't know what to do. I knew it would take me two days to climb back down, and I'd never get to my grandfather in time. Everybody left, and I was alone and completely freaked out on the mountain. Then a black cat stepped out of a cave and walked up to me. I could tell it didn't want to be seen by the others. It called me over and suggested I parachute down the mountain. It pointed to a parachute and then to a small speck at the base of the mountain and said that was the hospital where my grandfather was dying. So I grabbed the parachute, clutched it to my chest, and leaped off the mountain.

"I was falling in slow motion, and I realized my parachute would never open at that speed. The ground was approaching slowly, but even so, I knew that I would die upon impact. I panicked and pulled the cord, but the chute just trickled out of the pack. I was free-falling in slow motion.

"Looking down again, I could see the building, and I recognized that it was a hospital because of a large red cross painted on the roof. As I got closer, the cross symbol started to transform into a sharp metal crucifix that was about ten feet tall and six feet wide. The building became a church. I was still falling in slow motion and kicking my feet and waving my arms, trying to change course because I was headed directly for the point of the cross. I slowly hit the crucifix feetfirst, but with sufficient force that I saw it penetrate the entire length of my body until it came out at the base of my neck. I was in enormous pain!

"In the next instant, I was standing outside the church looking up at myself impaled on the crucifix. I was sort of squirming like a worm on a fishhook trying to get free. I heard a tapping sound next to me and noticed an old, dust-covered stained glass window. I cupped my hands around my eyes to look in and saw my grandfather's face staring blankly at me. He didn't say anything, but I could see that he was crying. I couldn't reach him. Then I looked up again in time to see myself gasp for one final breath before dying. And then I noticed the black cat from the mountain. It was now crouching on the roof right below my crucified body. It just glared at me for a moment and then started laughing. That's when I woke up," he concluded.

I gave Dennis time to regain his composure before commenting, "I'm sorry. That's a pretty disturbing nightmare to endure, especially for as long and often as you have. Before it slips out of your mind, can you describe any emotions you feel as you're telling it to me?"

"I guess I feel scared because I've kicked my sheets and blankets off the bed trying to get loose from the cross, but I feel more guilty than anything," he replied. "Does that make any sense that I'd feel guilty about dying in my own dream?"

"It's not important that your dream makes sense to me," I cautioned. "It's important that we connect your dream to what's going on in your life so that it makes sense to you. Let's peel back some of the layers and take a look at what your dream is revealing," I said encouragingly. "The first noteworthy symbol popped up right at the start when you found yourself hiking. Interestingly enough, hiking is a common dream symbol that often means the same thing to many people. What does hiking mean to you?"

Dennis looked at his feet for a moment as if imagining his hiking boots before stating that he thought it meant exploring or taking a journey. I complimented him and told him that now we could be sure that the dream centered on a journey. Then I told him I was going to need a little help with the name of the dormant volcano that sounded like a Pokemon cartoon. He laughingly replied and repeated the name "Paektu-san."

"Whatever. I need to know if this area holds any significance to you. What is it about the dormant volcano that interested you while you were in Korea?" I asked.

"Well, it interested me on two levels. First, it's a volcano and the highest mountain in Korea, but I was also interested because it used to be a site of human sacrifices," Dennis replied. "Tribes living in the area used to offer sacrifices to their various gods by delivering those they believed to be possessed into the volcano," he explained.

"Then the dream image we have so far is of you venturing out on a journey to the highest mountain in Korea. The mountain denoted danger in that it was safe for the time being, but as a volcano, it could turn deadly at any time. We should also pay attention that the mountain may have represented a spiritual quest to get closer to God.

"Now let's take a look at what happened on the mountain. You encountered a group of missionaries, one of whom was the missions leader from your church," I continued. "It would help if you could tell me about your relationship with him in order to put some pieces together."

"He's an old family friend who actually talked me into this mission to Korea in the first place. He's a great guy. My dad and he have been like brothers since college. In fact, he knew my grandpa pretty well," Dennis replied.

"I understand. Then your dream took on an additional theme where your missions leader warned that there was an emergency at home and you needed to get back. You knew that it was your grandfather, even though no one told you so," I commented. "Stepping out of the dream for a moment, Dennis, is your grandfather alive?"

"No, he passed away from a heart attack about two years ago," he said sadly.

"That explains why, in your dream, you knew your grandfather was having a heart attack, but let's get back to your dream. The next thing that happened was the appearance of the mysterious cat who just sort of showed up on the mountain," I continued. "Did you have a cat as a pet, or did anyone you've stayed with recently have a cat?" I asked.

"No . . . no cats. I don't have a clue what it had to do with my dream. I just knew that it was avoiding the group of missionaries," he finished.

"So the next image in your dream had the cat speaking to you and pointing out a parachute, suggesting that it was the best way to get down the mountain quickly. It also pointed to a speck where your grandfather was in the hospital."

He nodded affirmatively.

"Did the cat have a male or female voice?" I asked.

"It didn't really talk," he replied. "I just sort of heard it think out loud."

"And then you grabbed the parachute and jumped off the mountain. Then you noticed that you were traveling in slow motion and recognized that the chute wouldn't open at that speed. Falling in slow motion is a symbol that you know danger is ahead. There's time to correct your course, but you don't want to or you feel *powerless* to change."

"I'm with you," he said suspiciously. "When are you going to tell me what this whole thing means?"

"Bear with me. We're almost there," I said. "And the next thing you knew you were plunging toward a hospital with a large red cross emblem on the roof, but as you got nearer, it turned into a sharp metal crucifix. Then you hit the cross feetfirst, it impaled you, and the top of the cross came out of your neck.

"Your next image was of yourself; we call that *mirroring.*"

Continuing slowly so we could both discern the meaning, I said, "In your dream, *mirroring* meant you were standing on the ground in front of the hospital *and* you were still impaled on the crucifix. Then the building changed into a church. You were standing outside, heard tapping on the glass, looked inside, and saw your grandfather's image through an old stained glass window. He was staring at you and crying."

"That's the part that tears me up inside, sir. He just looked so sad. I could tell he was disappointed in me," Dennis said, looking down as though sensing shame. "Then he died."

"These dream symbols and themes are about as complex as I've encountered, but I think we can make sense of them," I said. "Because you are hiking up this volcanic, postsacrificial mountain, let's call the theme: Dennis's dangerous spiritual journey. You met a cat on the mountain that was avoiding the missionaries—," I said, stopping midsentence. "What type of cat?"

"I don't know. It was just a black cat," Dennis answered.

"Close your eyes and look at it again through your mind's eye. Is there anything distinctive about the cat?" I asked.

Pondering and cocking his head to the side, Dennis announced in a self-satisfied tone, "It's one of those cats with the slanted, almond-shaped eyes. What are they called?" his voice raised slightly.

"You mean a Siamese cat?" I asked.

"Yeah, that's what it was—a Siamese cat," he exclaimed. "But why is it important what type of cat it was?"

"You tell me, Dennis," I replied. "When you think of a Siamese cat, is it male or is it female?"

"Definitely female."

"Right," I agreed. "I don't know why I didn't see it earlier. Here's where it all fits together and what your dream is revealing."

Collecting my thoughts, I took a deep breath and began, "Your trip to Korea was a dangerous spiritual journey. You started out connected to your missionary comrades, but something happened along the way that caused you to separate emotionally or spiritually from them. The Siamese cat on the mountain suggested that you met a woman in Korea. Because the cat was halfway up the mountain, it suggested she started on the spiritual journey with you, but then she stopped for whatever reason. Then because the cat avoided your comrades, I'm guessing she wasn't a Christian, or you projected somehow that she felt unwelcome among your group.

"How are we doing so far?" I asked.

With a sheepish expression, Dennis replied that he wanted to tell me something, but that it was not to be told to his father or anyone at his church. I assured him that anything he told me was in confidence.

"I did meet a Korean girl who showed up in one of our Bible studies with a couple of friends," Dennis said with a look of embarrassment. "We really hit it off, and I actually had strong feelings for her. She spoke a little English and came back several times to our Bible study group. I was witnessing to her alone after a meeting one night, and we went out for something to eat. I don't want to get into the details, but one thing led to another and things got out of hand. I just let my emotions run away with me.

"The rules are clear. We're not supposed to date the locals and especially not the daughter of a Buddhist government official. The next thing I knew, I was yanked into a confrontation with her father and their Buddhist priest, and they were telling me that if I didn't leave their country immediately, my life would be ruined. I don't even know what they meant by ruined, but I didn't wait around to find out," he said dejectedly.

"And what became of the Korean girl after that?" I asked.

"I wrote her a note telling her I was sorry for what happened. She wrote back saying her father told her that I was using her for my own sexual deviancy. He told her I was using religion to weaken her emotionally and that that's how Americans lure young girls away from their faith. She told me not to contact her again," he replied.

"Now the dream makes absolute sense, Dennis," I said quietly. "The girl who appeared as the cat symbol directed you off her mountain. In your confused emotional state of mind, she appeared ambiguous. On the one hand, she told you to take a flying leap, but on the other, she handed you a parachute.

"As you fell from the mountain, which represented your spiritual journey, you did so in slow motion because you were feeling emotionally torn and powerless. Part of you wanted to stay on the mountain with her, but part of you knew you had to go because you were headed for a big fall. You did what you had to do, which was to leap from the mountain and begin your descent. Then you hit the crucifix feetfirst and became impaled. Metaphorically this was your mind's way of dealing with the stress of believing you had been tried and convicted and would be crucified when you got home.

"Now about the disturbing image of your crying grandfather in the church window. Am I close to target by guessing he was a deeply religious man?" I asked.

He admitted that was true. His grandfather had been a missionary, as had been his father.

"So then your grandfather's image in the church window is your projection of how seriously you've let him and your father down," I commented.

"That's why what happened was so out of control! I've disgraced my family! Three generations of missionaries, and I'm the first to have an inappropriate relationship with a local. That's a testimony I'll carry with me for the rest of my life," Dennis lamented.

After a moment, Dennis added, "Look, I'm sorry, but I haven't been completely honest with you. You're not the first doctor I've told my dream to. I got so distraught over these dreams and I got so little sleep that I went to an M.D. for sleeping pills. I ended up telling him about my dreams, and he actually made some of the connections you made. Well, at least he connected that I was under a lot of anxiety because I had to leave Korea. Anyway, he prescribed sleeping pills and something for anxiety that I've been taking for a little while. The problem is that they're not helping. I still have these dreams, and I'm still a nervous wreck."

"Then my question back to you is, If you already connected your dreams to your Korean experience, then why did you come to see me?" I inquired.

"I don't know why. I already presumed my nightmares were about how I messed up in Korea. I didn't know what each symbol meant, but even now that I do, I really don't see the point. No offense, but this doesn't change anything that happened. My nightmares aren't going to stop just because I told you about them. I think all that happened is that one more person knows what an idiot I am . . ." He trailed off.

"That's quite a pity party you're throwing for yourself, huh?" I asked.

"I don't have to do this," he said as he stood and began moving toward the door.

"You're right, you don't have to do this," I agreed. "You can walk out the door and ignore the possibility that spiritual warfare is being waged over you."

Dennis froze in his tracks, turned slowly, and asked, "What do you mean, 'spiritual warfare'?"

"Just that it isn't uncommon for missionaries to report odd occurrences where they feel as though Satan has been toying with or tempting them. Even more so while they are actively preaching and witnessing to non-Christians. If you believe in God, then you must believe in Satan, and Scripture is very clear that Satan disrupts Christians whenever he's given an opportunity."

"I didn't think of this in terms of spiritual warfare," Dennis said thoughtfully.

"No offense, Dennis, but then you were either ill-prepared or naive. You went to Korea to serve God. While you were there, you stumbled. That's not up for debate. What is debatable now is, Who is going to claim victory?" I questioned.

"What do you mean, 'claim victory'?" he replied.

"If there are only two teams on the field, God's team and Satan's team, then who's cheering and feeling victorious at the moment? Which team is thrilled to death that you came home with your tail between your legs, ready to give up?"

"I get your point," Dennis said as he nodded his head slowly. "So you're saying that if I get my head screwed on straight and get back to God's work, then I haven't really failed?" he asked.

"That's what I'm saying. Look, I know it seems that you're the first and only Christian guy who ever had to live with an indiscretion on your ledger, but I assure you that you are not. And as for how your grandfather in heaven is handling this, you are projecting harsh thoughts that I'm certain are not the case. I'm not trying to minimize your indiscretion—you messed up—but the quicker you understand how it happened, repent, and resolve not to let it happen again, the quicker God can use you again.

"If you recall in Paul's letter to the Romans, he took great care to describe what it was like to be a human, sinful man. He eloquently relayed how he struggled to resist doing things he *knew* he shouldn't do. Paul came to the conclusion that the Christian life is destined to be an ongoing struggle between doing what is right and holy versus doing what our sinful nature, or Satan, tempts us to do [Rom. 7:14–23]," I concluded.

EPILOGUE

Whether it is the sheer uncomfortableness of talking about our dreams, or the fact that they seem so bizarre and sometimes even psychotic, most people feel a need to reassert their normalcy. As with Dennis, let me go on record as saying, dreams are weird and borderline psychotic by nature. Some of the strangest dreams I have heard have come from some of the most normal, spiritually grounded people I've met.

I followed up with Dennis for a period of about six weeks and helped him deal with the consequences of his choices. To his credit, he stepped up and told the people he needed to tell the truth and handled the moderate disciplinary action handed down by his church with maturity and grace.

Although he continued to have vivid dreams prior to the disciplinary action taken by his church, he did not have the recurring nightmare again. At the time of this writing, Dennis had enrolled in seminary with a goal of attaining his master's degree in divinity and becoming a pastor.

CASE NOTES:

A Visitor from Her Grave

NAME: Randi
AGE: 23
OCCUPATION: Department store clerk
MARITAL STATUS: Married 8 years, with 1 child (age 7)

When organized religion, otherwise known as church, is done well, it is one of the richest experiences we can have. The friendships, connections, and support we receive from others within the church body, especially in Sunday school and other smaller groups, are beneficial in countless ways. On the other hand, when church is done poorly, it can be about as emotionally damaging as anything you can imagine.

I received a call from Dr. Curtis, MFCC (marriage, family, and child counselor), who had heard me talking about dreams and the Bible on a local radio program. She related that she had been working with a patient named Randi for approximately three months. Their efforts, to date, had primarily centered on Randi's separation from her husband, who had been physically and emotionally abusive. Dr. Curtis asked if I could meet with Randi regarding a series of dreams that she'd been having. She added that her patient had spoken with her pastor about the dreams and that his interpretation surprised the two of them. I agreed to meet with Randi the following day.

After settling into her seat, Randi told me that she came to my office expecting one of two things from a Christian doctor who analyzes dreams. I'd be some Freudian-looking guy who would say only "aah-haa" for the entire hour before blaming it on her mother, or I'd be sitting in an office full of incense and candles. Zero for two was my reply.

Stating the obvious, I said, "So, Dr. Curtis tells me you've been having some recurring dreams?"

"Yes, I've been having this one dream in particular that's really got me confused, as if my life weren't confusing enough already," she said, smiling.

"How often do you have the dream?" I asked.

"I've had some horrible dreams in the last six months, but nothing in comparison to the two dreams that I want to tell you about today. I've probably had this nightmare twice in the last ten days. But the part that gets me is that it sticks around. I awaken frozen in fear, and there's no getting back to sleep. Then the memory lingers with me for days. In the morning I'm angry at the world and especially at my husband. I know I have to forgive him, but I can't find it in my heart to do it."

"What are you trying to forgive him for?" I inquired.

"I've been in an abusive marriage since the start," she began. "At first he would just put me down verbally, but over the past six months to a year, he's started hitting me."

"Have you called the police?" I asked.

"No, but I did talk to our pastor about it. He met with my husband and things got better for a short time after that, but then it started up again," she replied.

"Did you receive any advice from your pastor about how to deal with an abusive husband?" I asked.

With a sigh Randi replied, "I know everyone's praying for me and our marriage, but I go to a very conservative church that doesn't allow separation at all, and divorce only under extreme conditions. My pastor counsels that the Bible is silent on the word *separation* in marriage; therefore, it is not allowed. There was one couple who divorced after the husband was caught having an affair. My church withdrew their membership and asked them to leave."

Noticing my blood pressure on the rise, I decided to avoid the subject of church doctrine. Instead I asked, "And did you tell him about the dreams you've been having?"

"Yes, and he told me that he thought God was speaking to me through my dream," she said. "That's why Dr. Curtis wanted me to come and see you.

Because I don't want to go against God's leading in any part of my life. My pastor told me that the woman who comes out of my grave in my dreams is me. He thought that God was using my dream to warn me to stay with my husband. He thought that doing anything but staying in and working on my marriage would cause me to become spiritually dead like that woman. Oh, there's one more issue. My pastor counseled me that I don't have scriptural grounds to either leave or divorce my husband. He warned that if I do, our church doctrine teaches that a divorced woman cannot get into heaven unless her ex-husband allows it. I know my husband, and if I divorce him, there's no way he's going to do anything but make me spend eternity in purgatory."

It was rapidly becoming clearer why Dr. Curtis referred Randi to me. We were dealing with church doctrine issues on top of the dreams. Not wanting to encroach on her pastor's area of expertise, I said, "You, Dr. Curtis, and I should get together and walk through the Scriptures relating to divorce so that you know exactly where you stand. In preparation for that meeting, you may also want to ask your pastor to point out where the Bible orders you to stay in a home with a husband who abuses you physically and emotionally. Divorce is one thing, but personal safety and sanity are distinctly different issues."

Directing her back to the purpose for this meeting, I said, "Why don't we focus on the recurring dream and see if we can make some sense of it? Do you feel up to telling me what you recall of this dream?"

"That's why I'm here," she replied. A silent minute passed while Randi closed her eyes and searched her memory for details about her dream. Opening her eyes, she calmly began to relate a dream that sounded more like a script for a horror movie than a dream.

Speaking slowly, she said, "My dream took place in the backyard of our home. My husband and I were asleep in bed when I heard a horrible commotion in our backyard. We have two German shepherds in real life. One is mine, the other is his, and they're in my dream too. I heard them barking and growling like there was an intruder in our yard. I tried to shake my husband awake, but he wouldn't wake up. I got out of bed and walked to the sliding glass door that led out to the backyard from our bedroom. Opening the blinds, I turned on the porch light and could see that our two dogs were standing over a freshly dug gravesite with a headstone. They were barking and growling at the ground over the grave as it started to shake, rise, and then crack open. First a hand, then an arm jutted from the grave. My husband's shepherd started biting and pulling large pieces of flesh from the arm while my dog barked but was more frightened than anything."

Drawing a deep breath, Randi continued, "I had this sensation that I should try to help this woman, but I was terrified of her at the same time. She emerged from the grave and I could see that she was beautiful once, but now she looked like death. She had rotting skin that split open to reveal broken bones, some missing teeth, and large clumps of hair, which had decayed and fallen out.

"The shepherds continued barking at the corpse while backing her into the corner of our yard. I felt like I had to do something, so I reached for a gun from my nightstand. I grabbed it and ran into the backyard. When I reached the woman, I lifted the revolver from my side to warn her to leave my dogs alone and get out of my yard, but my gun had turned into a book.

"I held the book up in front of me, and it frightened the woman. All of a sudden she looked weak and pitiful, and I wasn't afraid of her anymore. Just then, my husband came out of the house, knocked the book from my hands, and began to beat the corpse with his fists. The woman fell and crawled back to her grave where she disappeared under the fresh soil. Without saying anything, my husband took the book and set it on top of the grave. Even though nothing was said, I could tell that the book had some power over keeping this woman from coming out of her grave again."

Randi then provided me with the surprise ending: "Finally my husband calmly walked back into the house, locked the door behind him, and got back into bed. I was locked out and left standing at the sliding glass door, looking in. I saw the corpse woman from the backyard, lying on one side of my husband while a second corpse of a woman was lying beside him on the other side. All were asleep and couldn't see me or hear me banging on the door to get in. That was when I woke up."

"And what emotions did you feel when you awakened from this dream?" I asked.

"That's what is so odd about these dreams," she said. "I was not as scared as I was angry. But why was I angry? The corpse woman didn't hurt anyone. I'm frustrated that I can't get into the house, and there are two corpses in bed with my husband. So I don't understand my rage. That's why I think God might be telling me something through my dream."

"I think your rage will become quite clear in a moment," I said confidently. "Let's look at this as if it were a play. The stage is set in act one. You and your husband were at home, asleep in bed. Being asleep in one's own bed often symbolizes the subconscious wish for everything to be normal, comfortable, to feel right. Your two German shepherds entered the scene when there was a commotion in your backyard. The German shepherds are important in that one is yours while the other is your husband's. This comes into play, as your husband's dog becomes the aggressor and attacker. The German shepherds also denote protection, being on guard, and watching.

"Next up, we saw the symbol of the backyard come into play. Backyards in dreams denote a sense of being close to home. Depending on what is happening in the backyard, it can take on a positive or a negative connotation. In your case, the backyard definitely relates to trouble lurking around the corner, or trouble is closer than you think. That said, when you heard a commotion in your backyard, it symbolized trouble sneaking up on you from where you least expected it. So let's summarize this first act of your play: you were sleeping in bed, hoping that everything was okay in your life and your marriage, but trouble was lurking right around the corner. With me so far, Randi?"

"Yes. I'm with you. Go on," she replied.

"In act two you tried to awaken your husband to alert him to the danger, but he wouldn't wake up. The way you tried to awaken your husband is an important symbol. I believe you said you shook him, but he wouldn't wake up. Trying to shake someone awake versus simply calling his name or touching him denotes anger, urgency, and desperation. His response tells us that consciously you viewed your husband as ignoring or being indifferent to your needs. Then your dream told me something that caught my attention. You mentioned opening the blinds to look outside. Do you have blinds in your bedroom?" I asked.

"No, we have curtains. I thought that was a bit odd, but what's the difference?" Randi asked with a shrug of her shoulders.

"The difference is significant," I suggested. "Window blinds are often metaphors for darkness, distance, and secrecy. Since the blinds were on your bedroom window, we have to look at bedrooms as dream symbols, which denote intimacy. So what you're telling me is that there is a shroud of darkness, distance, and secrecy surrounding intimacy in your life. The commotion in the backyard was trying to break through the shroud of secrecy."

She nodded that she understood before I went on.

Continuing, I said, "Now the third act began when you turned on the outside light . . ."

"And that was my mind's way of trying to see what was posing a threat?" she asked.

"Very good," I affirmed. "Then your two dogs were standing over a gravesite with a headstone. Graves in dreams denote something that has died emotionally inside you, but hold that thought for a moment. Next, the ground shook and rose, and then a hand, followed by an arm, came out of the grave. This scene is rich in metaphor in that a little of the arm came out at a time. This tells us that the parts of you that are emotionally dead were trying to be seen in the hope of receiving help.

"Your husband's dog bit and pulled the flesh from the corpse's arm. It seems significant to me that it is your husband's dog that attacked the corpse and not yours. This will clear up for you in a moment. Then the corpse emerged from the grave, and you saw that it was a woman. You were still afraid, but you noticed that she was frightened too. You could see that she was beautiful once, but now she was rotting and decaying. I'll tie that loose end up in a moment.

"Act four began as you took a gun out of your nightstand. Guns are noteworthy in women's dreams because they suggest hostility, resentment, and sometimes jealousy. If we are beginning to infer that you are the corpse woman, then by virtue of your removing a gun from your nightstand, we might conclude that you have had some desperate and perhaps even some suicidal thoughts during this ordeal," I said, pausing to catch Randi's eyes.

"I have had some feelings that felt desperate enough to make me think about suicide. Dr. Curtis and I have talked about that extensively, and I've given her my word that I would never do such a thing. You're right, though, in that I've thought about it," she announced.

"Thank you for your candor and for dealing with those feelings with Dr. Curtis," I commended her. "Guns as a general dream symbol also denote feelings of anger, suspiciousness, and perhaps jealousy.

"Still in this act, you, as the corpse, have been backed into a corner of your yard. This image suggests you felt trapped and helpless in your marriage.

The gun you were carrying turned into a book, which was an interesting little twist I've never encountered in a dream before. A book as a dream symbol usually connects to rules, laws, wisdom, or authority. Because this book transformed from a hostile and deadly symbol—i.e., the gun—into a book, it suggests the book may be the reason you're feeling trapped in a corner. I'm going to take a calculated guess that the book was a Bible. We can verify it easily," I said, pausing. "Do you have a Bible on your nightstand?"

"Yes. As a matter of fact I do have one in my nightstand," she replied.

"What about a gun?" I inquired.

"I don't like guns, but my husband keeps a gun in the nightstand on his side of the bed," she said.

"Then it's pretty clear to me that you were holding a Bible up to the corpse version of yourself," I asserted.

"But why would I be afraid of the Bible?" she asked.

"It's not that you are afraid of the Bible per se. It's that you were feeling trapped or backed into a corner by what's in the Bible or who is standing behind the Bible's authority. Bibles occasionally show up as a dream symbol for marriage, which also fits here. You could be asserting you feel trapped and helpless in your marriage," I suggested.

"Still with me?" I asked.

She assured me that she was and that this was making a lot of sense to her.

"Now in act five of six total, your husband's dog bit you as the corpse woman. Again, it wasn't your dog that attacked, but your husband's. This further proves that you're the corpse woman. In your dream you said that you could tell that the corpse woman, once beautiful, was now starting to decay. These are all real-life metaphors for how dead, drawn out, and emotionally straining this experience has been on you.

"Still in the fifth act, your husband appeared and grabbed the book/Bible from you and beat you/the corpse woman with his fists, which drove her back into her grave. Continuing the thought that you are the corpse woman, why would your husband grab a Bible from your hands and hit you?" I asked suspiciously.

"That's easy for me to discern," she replied. "He hates it when I quote the Bible to him as the authority that what he is doing is wrong. He hates it when

I talk with other Christians about him, and most of all, he hates it that I use Scripture to try to get him to be a better husband."

"Since we've established you are the corpse woman," I said calmly, "let's see what she's trying to tell us. When your husband grabbed the Bible out of your hand, again, that registered your unconscious fear that he may have God and the church behind him. In your dream, you were sent back to your grave by the Bible, so in real life, it could be that you feel silenced and dismissed by those in the church.

"On to our final act," I continued. "In your dream you found yourself locked outside while your husband went back to bed. This stirs an image of being on the outside looking in and, more important, not knowing what's going on. This certainly fits the helpless feelings you've described. And finally you looked inside and you saw yourself, as the corpse woman, in bed with your husband, but you were sharing your marriage bed with another corpse. Your husband, yourself as the corpse woman, and the second corpse woman are all asleep. This strikes me as a suspicion floating into your dream," I said. "Do you have concerns that your husband is having an affair?"

"I didn't until about two weeks ago when I got a phone call from an anonymous woman telling me he was," Randi replied.

"I understand, and I'm sorry, Randi. Have you shared that with Dr. Curtis?" I asked.

"Yes, she's aware of it," she said.

"Then it's better for us to leave those issues between you and your doctor and stick to the dream material here," I suggested.

"That makes sense," she said with a sigh. "I guess my pastor was right about the dead woman in my dreams being me. Then he might also be right that God is sending me a message that I can't even have a trial separation from my husband."

"Your pastor was correct about you being the corpse woman. I mean no disrespect, but occasionally even a blind squirrel finds an acorn," I said, smiling. "You came to me in search of answers. One answer related to the meaning of your recurring dream. I think we've established that your dream is an accurate drama featuring all of your marriage anxieties.

"But now to consider the question of whether your pastor is right about your dream being divinely sent," I said. "It's always possible, but I don't think so. I can generally discern whether a dream is divinely inspired by passing it through three question filters. The first filter is a *revelation filter.* By asking, Did the dream reveal facts that could not have been known to the dreamer? we get a glimpse of the dream's origin. In your case, it seems that each act of your dream drama was already known to you or at least suspected.

"I call the second filter *inspired direction.* Through this filter we search the dream for a sign that God may be directing you to take some *unusual* action that you have not considered. Again, in the case of this dream, it reveals known or subconscious facts, but it doesn't seem to be providing a course of action," I said.

"The third filter is a *scriptural filter.* I use this when a dream does produce a clear direction to the dreamer. I take that direction, check it against Scripture, and then examine whether the dream direction coincides with biblical truth. If it doesn't, then we should not interpret it to be inspired. Your pastor interprets your dream to mean God is telling you to stay in your home and endure your situation. Even after you told him that your husband is physically and emotionally abusive, his advice remained the same, right?" I asked.

"Yes, he said I don't have biblical grounds to leave," she replied.

"Well, again, I mean no disrespect to your pastor, but we're not talking about divorce here. We're talking about your safety, and you have every scriptural right to separate from your husband for safety's sake. You may want to ask your pastor which of the following he believes the case to be: Is your husband's abusiveness simply because he's hotheaded and a little reckless, or are his actions immoral or even evil? If he minimizes what is happening and says your husband is just a little hotheaded and reckless, then take him lovingly to Proverbs 14:16, which reads: 'A wise man fears the LORD and shuns evil, but a fool is hotheaded and reckless.' On the other hand, if he agrees that abuse is evil, then walk him through 2 Timothy 2:22, where we're instructed to flee evil. If all else fails, ask him if abuse jibes with Ephesians 5:28 instructing husbands to love their wives as they love themselves.

"So, Randi," I continued, "I think your pastor is wrong in interpreting your dream to be divinely inspired, and I think he is wrong in suggesting you must stay and endure abuse. This simply doesn't wash with Scripture."

EPILOGUE

Randi seemed satisfied with my interpretation of her dream, and she returned to Dr. Curtis for continued support with her marital crisis. Dr. Curtis called about six weeks later to tell me that much had changed in a short period of time. Randi's husband was caught red-handed and finally admitted he was having an affair. He compounded that mistake by moving in with his girlfriend.

Randi advised her pastor that not only did she have biblical grounds for divorce, but that she had a restraining order and had started divorce proceedings. Dr. Curtis concluded by asking me to explain something she didn't understand about Christians. Apparently the pastor had found out that Randi's husband was living with his girlfriend and that he had, in fact, emotionally and physically abused Randi. Because of that, the pastor and elders of the church revoked the couple's church membership and asked both to leave the congregation. Dr. Curtis inquired about why a church would do that. I acknowledged to Dr. Curtis that all too often, Christians shoot their wounded rather than tend to their wounds. And as for *why*, the only answer I could provide was that I think the church panics over perceived imperfections and is afraid whatever virus these imperfect people have could be contagious and spread to the rest of the congregation.

Dr. Curtis said that it is times like these that make her happy she's an agnostic. I suggested we talk again soon.

CASE NOTES:

Death on the Operating Table

NAME: Victor
AGE: 56
OCCUPATION: Orthopedic surgeon
MARITAL STATUS: Married 28 years

One question I am often asked during interviews is, "Of all the dreams you've interpreted, do you have a favorite?" Even though dozens come to mind, one distinct dream always leads the pack.

Victor and I worked at the same hospital, yet our paths seldom, if ever, crossed. While I was working on the fourth-floor psychiatric unit, Victor was on the first floor, part of the surgery unit, and enjoyed the reputation of being one of the finest orthopedic surgeons in the country. I can recall talking to Victor only three times in three years: once at a hospital administration meeting, once while trying to figure out what a particular cafeteria food was, and once as he was sneaking a cigarette in the parking structure. On that occasion Victor tipped his hand about his appreciation for the field of psychology by telling me, "Don't tell anyone that I smoke, Dr. Head Shrinker." He said this through a thick Middle Eastern accent and without a trace of a smile.

"Your secret's safe with me, Marlboro Man," I replied, smiling and faking a cough.

I wasn't even sure how much English Victor spoke until he called me a week after the garage encounter.

"Head Shrinker, this is Victor," he announced—as if anyone else referred to me by that name.

"Marlboro Man," I replied. "To what do I owe this honor?"

"I hear talk you are a religious man, no?" he asked. I admitted that I was indeed. He proceeded to ask if I did psychological seminars on dreams as he had heard. I admitted that was true as well.

"I had a horrible dream three nights ago and then had the same horrible dream last night. If I come down and visit you in one hour, you can tell me what it means, no?" he asked.

"No," I said. "I've got patients to see. I can work you in at four P.M. Come on down and I'll see you then."

"Four P.M.?" he asked in an exasperated tone. "I leave the hospital at two."

Playing dumb, I said, "Great, Doctor. That'll give you plenty of time to get back to my office by four."

"Very well. Four P.M. it is," he snapped. "Oh, and . . . uh, thanks."

At precisely 4:00 P.M., Victor walked into my waiting room. I greeted him and invited him to come into my office.

"It's nice to see you again, Doctor," I said in my most professional tone. "How can I help you?"

"Before I tell you anything, Head Shrinker, you will promise me it is confidential," he said sternly.

I assured him it would be completely confidential.

"As I said on the phone, I've had two dreams, the first three nights ago and again last night. You will tell me what they mean, no?" he questioned.

"I'll do my best, Doctor. Why don't you sit down and fill me in on your dream, and I'll see what I can do?" I answered.

"Very well. Two dreams . . . but both with the same meaning. As I said, one three nights ago, and then again last night. I do not wish to talk about God. I am a surgeon and a scientist. But I have never before had two identical dreams like these. Nor have I ever had the same dream twice that I recall. This is why I looked you up. You are the writer of religious psychology books, no?" he questioned.

"Yes, I've written a few from the position of a Christian therapist," I answered. "But help me to understand why it's important to you that the person who hears your dreams is religious, Victor."

"Because a colleague says that I am being visited by God. I say he is crazy, and he says I should come ask you. Here I am. Now you tell me," Victor said.

"Okay. Let's start at the top. Tell me about your dream, and please don't spare any detail, even if you think it is meaningless," I cautioned.

"Very well. By the way, how much does this cost me?" Victor said with a half smile and a half-suspicious look on his face.

"Triple what it costs everyone else if you don't get started," I replied. "Plus ten percent because I have to deal with your accent," I added with a smile. "Now get on with the dream, will you?"

"Yes. My dream starts with me in the hospital. I was scrubbing and getting ready to do a surgery on a friend's torn anterior cruciate ligament. That's the vertical strand of ligament fibers that runs diagonally through—"

"As riveting as this is, I'm not really seeing how this anatomy lesson will help us get through your dream, Victor," I interrupted.

"Forgive me, Head Shrinker, I will get on with my dream," he quipped. "As I said, I was scrubbing to do an ACL. I went into the operating room, and he was prepped and ready to go. I did the procedure just like I've done a thousand times in real life. As I was closing the site, I saw a bright light coming from the ceiling, and I could hear a voice," he recounted with a puzzled look on his face.

"What was the voice saying?" I asked.

"It was very hard to distinguish what he was saying, but I could tell that it was a man's voice and that it was coming from the bright light. Although I could not hear each word clearly, I was sure he was warning me about something. The next thing I knew, I was not the doctor in the operating room any longer. I had traded places with my patient, and he was about to perform open-heart surgery on me. I was floating above the table and looking down at myself as the surgeon and his team operated on me. I could hear them talking and saying that my heart was so occluded . . . oh, sorry, that means blocked . . . that they were surprised that I wasn't dead already. Then the doctor said, 'Time is short. Let's finish this before it's too late,'" he recounted.

"And then what happened?" I asked.

"They started to reroute a valve into my heart, but then I went into cardiac arrest. I was still hovering above my body, and I could see that my blood pressure was bottoming out and that they were losing me fast. I was scared, and all of a sudden I saw several of my family members who had died. They were standing around the table, crying and pleading with the doctors to save my life. It was no use, though; I died on the table. The last thing I saw before I awakened from my dream was the underside of the sheet that had been pulled over my head."

"Fascinating dream, Doctor," I commented. "You mentioned you were scared in your dream. What were you feeling when you awakened from the dream?"

"I was terrified like I had visited a ghost," he replied.

"Let me ask you a couple of questions to help me in discerning your dream, Doctor. The first is about the friend you are operating on in your dream. Do you recognize this friend?" I asked.

"Of course I recognize him," he tersely replied. "It was my friend Dr. Paul Petropolous. We went to medical school together, and he was my dearest friend as well as a brilliant surgeon."

"Just out of curiosity, what is Dr. Petropolous's medical specialty?" I inquired.

"Not *is*," he corrected. "*Was.* Sadly my friend has passed away. Two years ago next August it will be. And to your question, he was the top heart specialist in our class."

"What did the doctor die from?" I asked.

"That was the . . . what is the word you people use . . . irony. That was the irony of it all. Here he was a master heart surgeon working sixty- and eighty-hour weeks. He didn't take very good care of himself, he smoked a little like me, and he died of a massive heart attack," replied the doctor.

"I'm sorry," I said sadly. "I need to ask you another question. Regarding the family members you saw in the operating room, other than the fact that they were deceased, is there anything else in common about them?"

Victor thought for a moment and shook his head slowly before stating, "I cannot think of a single thing they had in common. There were both men and women. They were all adults. There were random people from one side of my family and some from another. By that I mean that not every dead member from either family was there. Just certain ones." He asked, "You tell me, Head Shrinker, is my colleague right? Is this a religious dream or just a nonsense dream?"

"Let's start with your friend, Victor. Correct me if I'm wrong, but I think we know three key things about him. First, he was your closest friend.

Second, he was a heart surgeon. And third, he died of a massive heart attack," I began.

"What does that tell us?" Victor interjected. "That tells us nothing!"

"Not so fast," I cautioned. "Let's get the results back before we issue a diagnosis."

"I'm sorry. Please continue," Victor said.

"The next thing you told me was that you were operating on your friend and you heard a man's voice. You were not sure what he was saying, but you could tell that he was warning you about something. You were also sure that the voice was coming from a bright light. There are three dream symbols in play here, Victor. The first was a man's voice, the second was the warning, and the third was that the voice was coming from a bright light. A bright light from above, in a Judeo-Christian's way of thinking, signifies God, knowledge, and wisdom. Because the male voice from above was indistinguishable in your dream, this could denote that you are acknowledging God's presence, but that you aren't tuned in to Him enough to understand the message. Last, the fact that the authoritative voice emanated from the light validates that, at least in your dream, you believed you were hearing a warning message from God." I paused before asking, "Victor, are you a religious man?"

"Ah, Head Shrinker, I knew we'd get around to that sooner or later. I am a nonpracticing Jew, and I have been to the synagogue only one time since my bar mitzvah, and that was to pick up my mother. Because I am not religious, doesn't that contradict your diagnosis that I am dreaming about God?" he inquired.

"Not at all, Doctor. I've tracked multiple divinely inspired dreams received by people with minimal, if any, religious beliefs. Just because an individual doesn't choose to acknowledge or worship God doesn't mean that God doesn't exist or that He turns His back on him," I assured him.

I tried to explain this more fully by encouraging him to think of it as taking a long drive into the country while listening to a favorite radio station. As you drive farther and farther away from the station, the signal begins to fade. Eventually you drive out of range and turn your radio off because all you hear is static. The radio station hasn't gone anywhere. It's still broadcasting loud and clear, but you'd have to go back to where you started to hear it again.

"Ah, I see what you did there. You make a nice little metaphor out of the radio being God and that I drove away from Him and that's why voices in my dream cannot be understood. I see what you did there," Victor said with a sly look. "Very nice, Head Shrinker."

"Your dream reminds me of dream symbols I've seen before. Dreams that have posed either health or safety warnings to religious people," I stated. I purposely did not tell Victor that in all of the cases, they seemed to be divinely inspired.

"Let's move ahead, Victor," I said. "The next symbol is that you have traded places with your patient. We now know that your patient was your doctor friend who died from a massive coronary. This would lead me to believe that you have some anxiety about your health. Victor, have you been experiencing any heart-related symptoms, or have you been worried about your health?"

"Not in the least!" he snapped defensively. "Oh, sure, I could stand to lose a few pounds and don't you even start about my smoking, but I am in great shape for a man my age."

"Just asking," I said apologetically. "Your next dream symbol found you having open-heart surgery. This connects back to the fact that you traded places with your friend, who died from a heart attack, and who is now operating on you.

"Next you related a floating, out-of-body experience where you became two Victors: one on the operating table and the other watching from a distance. Where, again, did you say you were in perspective to your body on the operating table?" I inquired.

"I was floating directly above my body, looking down on it," Victor replied.

"I see. The second Victor's vantage point is very important. In this case, you have the overhead view, which to the secular analyst means taking the position of authority. Over the years, however, I've come to understand a differing interpretation from both religious people and those who are struggling with issues of faith and religion. Like yours, in these dreams, the out-of-body image is floating above the real-life person. This suggests a barrier or obstacle between the real-life person and God," I said.

"Are you with me so far?" I asked with a smile.

He assured me that he was very interested and that I should continue.

"Your next symbol came when you heard your surgeon friend talking about how blocked, or occluded, your arteries were and how they were surprised you weren't already dead. This symbol has a dual meaning. The obvious one represents your conscious anxiety that you are not taking care of yourself physically," I said. "The other, more spiritual meaning is that you are closed off to faith, religion, and God. In your case, Victor, I'd consider both interpretations for the time being."

"I will admit that I've had a few fleeting thoughts about getting on in my age. Do you know what I mean, Head Shrinker? When you start to question what comes next?" he said with a softening tone of voice for the first time.

"I know exactly what you mean, Victor," I acknowledged. "I do that as well. But for me, it is with the firm assurance that I know where my *next* is. The symbol that follows in your dream bolsters the case that your dream is about health concerns and ultimately where your *next* will be.

"In your dream, you were floating between your body and God, and you heard your doctor friend say that time was short and that they must hurry before it was too late. This denotes some urgency in your life that you are running out of time to do something. Again, the recurring theme points to one of two things, or both. The first is getting your physical life in order while the second is getting your spiritual life in order," I said.

"And what about the sad scene with my deceased family members standing around me on the operating table upon my death? Why are they present, Doctor?" Victor asked in an almost pleading tone.

For the record, I noted that Victor had just referred to me as *doctor* instead of his usual barb. In therapeutic terms, that told me I had broken through his defenses and was earning his trust. I said, "Victor, there is a reason your deceased relatives are in the room, but you hold the key to unlock that secret. They appear to be a random selection of relatives, but there must be a connection in your subconscious. Search your memory to see if they were connected by the way they died, where they lived or died, their character, or religious beliefs. Something binds these people together in your mind, Victor."

"I cannot think of it at this moment. Later I will ponder that question until I find the answer," he said with determination. "That is the end of my dream because that is when I died."

"Actually the very end of your dream presented a gold nugget for us to examine," I corrected. "You did in fact die, but the irrationality of dreams allows us to experience something as final as death, but then continue to view the dream as though the death were just a minor element. In this case, you died, but you remained alert as you saw the sheet being pulled over your eyes. This symbol means a couple of important things. First, it speaks to me that subconsciously you acknowledge that you are worried about your health, but the sheet being pulled over your eyes while you are still alive denotes you are blind, or ignoring these concerns."

Leaning back in my chair to collect my thoughts, I continued, "The second and more abstract interpretation starts with your body appearing dead to everyone, while actually you are still alive. In this interpretation the key symbols are that you appear dead, but you are alive, your eyes, and the sheet that covers them. These symbols speak strongly to me that your subconscious acknowledges that you appear spiritually dead, but underneath there is a sleeping spirituality that wants to emerge. The sheet represents your life of spiritual blindness and a fear that it is too late. In your dream you see that the sheet has been pulled over your head. This means time has run out, and even though you are still alive, you have no physical power left to remove the sheet. And in your dreams, Victor, what do you see from underneath the sheet?" I asked.

Closing his eyes while looking slightly upward, Victor thought for a moment and then replied, "I see a soft light filtering through the sheet."

"Precisely," I said encouragingly. "Light from above in a dream often denotes spirituality and God's presence. Therefore, you are physically alive because you can faintly feel God's image through the sheet, but this is as close as you will get to reaching God.

"Are you on overload, Victor, or can you fit one more supporting piece of evidence that we are onto the right interpretation here?" I asked.

He assured me he was fine and asked for more evidence.

"It was your heart. A heart as a dream symbol denotes life, love, and spirituality. It's easy to presume that the fact that you are having a heart bypass is strictly a health concern, but it also has a spiritual connotation. Let me ask you, for a person to live a spiritual life, does he accept God into his heart or his head?"

"I believe it is both," replied Victor.

"And I agree with you. Therefore, because the sheet has been pulled over your head, you have no way to internalize God into your heart. Perhaps the meaning connected to your heart problem is that you are not able to get God past your head and into your heart," I offered.

Victor leaned back in his chair and stared blankly for nearly a minute before asking, "What is your recommendation?"

"Victor, I know you are a man who likes to hear the truth, so I'm going to give it to you straight. If I were the one having the dreams you've had, I would immediately schedule a complete physical, including a body scan of my heart to see if there was any reason for concern," I said.

"Do you mean you would place stock in the divine possibility of this dream to the extent that you see it is a warning sign?" he asked more inquisitively than accusingly.

"I believe in being safe rather than sorry, Victor. Humor me. If you have a physical and everything checks out, then maybe we're not dealing with a divinely inspired dream, and we'll go from there. We'll never know until you've had the physical," I added.

"You win, Doctor. There is no harm in having a physical. I will make an appointment with a colleague, and then I will come back next Wednesday again at four P.M. No?"

"Four P.M. Wednesday it is, Victor," I replied.

"Before I go, how about a little wager? I'll bet the amount I owe you for this session, double or nothing, that I am in perfect health," he said with a challenging smile.

"Now what kind of Christian example would I be setting for you if we gambled over your health?" I replied with a smile. "Save your money and buy a nicotine patch. I'll see you Wednesday."

‖   ‖   ‖

Victor came in at precisely 4:00 P.M. the following Wednesday. He sat down and smiled the smile of a man who had received a clean bill of health.

"So, Doctor, I surmise from your smile that it is a good thing I didn't bet with you about your health," I said.

"Actually my good Doctor Head Shrinker, you would be sitting on double your fees had you bet me," Victor replied. "I had my physical, and I am scheduled for a percutaneous transluminal coronary procedure—that's angioplasty for you head shrinkers—next Monday."

I was speechless for the first time that I could recall in quite a while. Finally I said, "What did the tests show?"

"They found a seventy-five percent blockage in the left main coronary artery and some atherosclerosi in other arteries. I am a walking time bomb, so do not upset me, no?" he said.

"Victor, I'm encouraged that you have this positive outlook and especially encouraged that you took your dream seriously enough to follow through on your physical. After you left my office last week, I didn't know if you would discount the entire dream scenario or not," I said.

"Oh, I wrestled with it for the next forty-eight hours, and I was just about to dismiss it as nothing more than two odd dreams until my wife reminded me of something. She remembered that my friend Dr. Petropolous was a deeply religious man. He was Greek Orthodox and attended Mass every Sunday and many times prior to coming to work at the hospital. There is no doubt in my mind that if there *is* a heaven, Dr. Petropolous has a front-row seat," he said with a hint of pride.

"Are you telling me that you think there is a possibility that your dream was divinely inspired and that God might be sending you a message through Dr. P. showing up in your dream?" I asked.

"Do not get a swelled brain, Doctor. There was one other fact that my wife pointed out," he said. "We talked about the deceased family members that I saw in my dream and she . . . ," Victor hesitated, and I could tell that he was fighting back tears, ". . . she is going to research it more, but she remembers at least three of these relatives being deeply religious."

I actually got a little choked up myself over Victor's revelation, but more so in solving a dream that seemed to be communicating a divine, life-saving message. "So, Victor, you're a logical, scientifically minded man. What's the plan?" I asked.

"Plan?" he said coyly. "My plan is to have my heart procedure and get back to work as soon as possible."

"Don't play coy with me, Victor," I admonished. "You know exactly what I'm talking about."

"Oh . . . you mean about the religious nature of my dream. Well, my wife and I discussed that at some length, and we've decided to attend church as soon as I am through with my operation," he replied.

"Don't take this the wrong way, Victor, but have you ever heard of fox-hole Christians?" I asked.

"No," he replied.

"Foxhole Christians is an old war expression, which means that all men become deeply religious when death is near. When the crisis is over, however, they go back to the way they were," I said.

"So you are worried that I am, how do you say . . . cutting a deal with God . . . to get me through my operation and then I will go back to the way I was?" he said.

I admitted that he had surmised my concern completely.

"I understand, Doctor Head Shrinker. That is why I will let you take me to lunch tomorrow. Maybe we can go to lunch the next day, too, so you can teach me how to accept God and to live as my friend Dr. Petropolous lived. You can even bill me for your time, unless you would like to go double or nothing," he concluded with a laugh.

"I think we can work something out," I replied.

Epilogue

There was little doubt in my mind that Victor's dream was divinely inspired. I have rarely seen such a clear combination of dream symbols all leading back to God. The question invariably arises, Why? Why does God send warning messages to some, while taking others without so much as a whisper? I think Solomon struggled with this paradox as mightily as anyone. In Ecclesiastes 7:15 he said,

> In this meaningless life of mine I have seen both of these:
> a righteous man perishing in his righteousness,
> and a wicked man living long in his wickedness.

I think Solomon ended up in the same position I have in pondering the question of why God does what He does. It's because He's in charge and He has the overhead view of our lives and all that surrounds them. God knows our future as well as our past. Therefore, He chooses accordingly. We have to take it on faith that God is not only sovereign, but that He loves us unconditionally.

Because of all these factors, whether we understand them or not, His decisions are always in our best interests.

In Victor's case, I wondered what plans God had for him. It's easy to say that Victor received a warning from God so that he could continue to do great things for his patients. Perhaps that is true, but I sense that God has much bigger plans for Victor than just what he can do in the operating room. Someday, I hope to have the luxury of asking God that question.

In the meantime, I connected Victor with a pastor I knew who had been a rabbi and converted to Christianity a number of years earlier. I also met with Victor three times prior to his surgery. During our final meeting, Victor triumphantly told me that he had accepted Christ at the encouragement of the pastor and that he and his wife would be attending church following his surgery.

Victor's surgery was a success, and he followed through on his pledge to attend church regularly. I bumped into him a few times over the next few months prior to my leaving the hospital for private practice. Each time he appeared happy and sincere in his faith. Our last encounter occurred in the basement of the hospital's parking garage. As I exited the stairway, I came across Victor enjoying a cigarette. He remarked with a wink, "Don't give me that look, Head Shrinker. Haven't you heard that Christians are not perfect, just forgiven?"

CASE NOTES:

A Forty-Year-Old Dream

NAME: Jack
AGE: Confidential
OCCUPATION: Christian television show host
MARITAL STATUS: Married

I was having lunch with an old friend whom I'd known since I was sixteen years old. About ten years my senior, Jack was an assistant store manager at the market where I worked as a box boy. Don't laugh. We all have to start somewhere.

During the relatively short time Jack and I worked together, we had very few conversations about God and religion, but I knew exactly where Jack stood as a committed Christian. That was fairly easy to recognize because while all the other non-Christian, or at least nonpracticing Christian, guys were unwinding after work with a few beers, Jack politely declined and headed home to his wife and kids.

Jack also knew where I stood on Christianity in those days. I was pretty certain there was a God, but I had to concentrate on playing high school baseball in hopes of cashing in on a college scholarship. I didn't have time for beer drinking, either, but my reluctance to join the guys had nothing whatsoever to do with God.

Over lunch we both agreed that thirty years have a way of clouding memories. Neither of us could remember the cause of our drifting apart. We did, however, narrow it down to three possibilities. One possibility was that Jack was transferred to another store. The second was that I left to play baseball. And the third, and most likely, was that management finally figured out I was the worst box boy in supermarket history and fired me.

In any event, while I was sacrificing my right arm to the baseball gods, Jack was charting an amazing course through life—a course that would lead to hosting one of the most popular Christian television programs of the 1980s and 1990s. Jack was, and continues to be, a major celebrity in Christian circles. During our most recent lunch, it was interesting to watch passersby recognize him and then try to decide whether they should interrupt him for an autograph.

While we were catching up on "old times," Jack asked what I was up to these days. When I mentioned that I was writing a book on dreams from a Christian perspective, Jack's eyes lit up. "Did I ever tell you that I came to accept Jesus as a result of a dream?" he asked.

"No," I replied, "but this is as good a time as any."

"I remember this dream as if it were yesterday, and I've even repeated it a few times on my program over the years. I was seventeen years old. My parents were both Christians and attended church somewhat regularly, but you know how it is with teenagers. I was enjoying a particularly worldly lifestyle at the time, and I really didn't want to give it up for anything, much less religion.

"I went to bed one night and had a dream that shook me to the core, so much so that I scrambled out of bed, hit my knees, and prayed to receive Christ that instant. My divine dream scared me so badly that I didn't take a moment to stop and consider that I was making a life-changing decision. It didn't matter because it was now or never," he recounted.

"I'm here to tell you that this dream was absolutely, positively divinely inspired, and it altered the course of my life. My dream opened with my getting ready for school early one morning. All of a sudden, I was stopped dead in my tracks, straining to identify a strange, overhead rumbling noise that started softly and then built to a massive crescendo. Looking up, I saw that the ceiling and roof over my room had disappeared. I stood frozen in amazement, looking straight up into the pitch-black sky and wondering what was going on. Suddenly storm clouds started to multiply, and the sky looked as though it would open up and pour rain at any moment. Just then, I was nearly knocked off my feet by a blinding bolt of lightning, followed by the sharpest clap of thunder I had ever heard. As quickly as they formed, the clouds parted, revealing a vast midnight blue opening from which descended the voice of God.

"God addressed me by name. He said that He had no time for small talk and that He had come to earth to make good on the promise He made in the book of Revelation. He told me it was time for Him to take believers home. He told me that He had already given me too much time and that I'd had many an opportunity to accept Him, but now it was too late. We both knew I'd procrastinated my decision simply so I could spend a while longer in my sinful lifestyle. God said how sorry He was that I would not be joining Him with my family. He told me I would be alone.

"In my dream I cried and pleaded with God to show me mercy, to give me just one more day to get my life in order. Relenting, God told me that He *would* grant me one final day, but there would be no further warnings or grace periods. Time had run out, and it was now or never for me," Jack continued.

"I awakened from my dream and found that I was so panicked and frightened that I was crying. I immediately prayed to God to forgive me of my sins and to come into my heart right then and there. I admitted that I was a sinner and asked Him if He would accept my soul, just as it was, at that time in my life.

"Greg, as sure as I'm sitting here with you right now, I felt God's answer. I turned warm and had a sensation that Someone was in the room with me. I know now that it was God who had entered my room and accepted my offering.

"I never fully understood what God was warning me about in my dream. I don't know if I was on a collision course with death or an accident. Perhaps He knew that I was headed down an impossible course through life, and had I not made the right decision that day, perhaps I never would. I only know that His message came through crystal clear. I had one final opportunity to accept Him before it was too late, and I wasn't about to let it pass me by," he concluded.

"So what does my dream mean, Greg?" he said sarcastically with a huge smile on his face. "And if you tell me that it was just a normal dream caused by eating some bad pizza, then you don't know jack—pun intended."

"I don't think I'd need Daniel's gifts to figure that one out," I said, referring to the dream interpretation Scriptures found in the book of Daniel. "Let me ask you something. You've been a Christian longer than I have. Is there any doubt in your mind that God spoke to you in your dream? I mean, isn't it possible that you were just feeling the guilt and pressure any young boy would feel among a family of Christians?" I asked.

"There is not even a possibility that it wasn't divinely inspired," he replied. "I'll tell you how I know. My life changed from that point forward. God began using me in ways I never even imagined He would. He brought me to this television ministry and handed me an opportunity to witness to millions of believers and nonbelievers. I believe God had a plan for my life, but I wasn't listening. The Scriptures reveal time and time again how God used dreams to grab someone's attention to do His will. I think my experience was just a modern-day version of God grabbing my attention through a dream, and I think it goes on all the time for people all over the world."

EPILOGUE

I find it impossible to second-guess Jack's divine accounting of his dream. If these same dream symbols were to pop up in my life or in the lives of others, I might have to look hard to get a sense of their origin. But based on the wonderful ministry Jack has provided over the last twenty-five years, how could anyone doubt that God used a vivid dream to command the attention of this tireless witnessing worker?

FAQs
(Frequently Asked Questions)

I hate computers! If you were to catch me at the wrong time, you might even find that I wouldn't cavalierly dismiss at least the possibility that one or more demons reside inside my computer. Indeed, one nasty little foul-tempered demon, whose sole responsibility is to make my life miserable, is undoubtedly System Error or Crash. The point of my tongue-in-cheek observation is that customer support can be a lifesaver, especially if the tech speaks English.

It's not that the 653-page manual that came with my computer isn't helpful. I'm sure it works for 2 percent of the population. It just doesn't happen to work for me. I find it infinitely more helpful to ask questions of another human being, although at times I wonder if I am actually speaking with a human being. So, if you are like me, it's always easier to get my mind around new concepts when I'm allowed to ask questions.

With this self-evident truth in mind I've assembled a few of the most common questions I receive in relationship to dreams along with abbreviated answers.

Note to reader: lest you believe I actually think a demon resides in my computer, I assure you, I do not. It's probably just a gremlin.

Q: What does the Bible say about dreams?
A: The Judeo-Christian tradition has long valued dreams and acknowledged God's use of them for divine revelation and other important communications. Dreams, visions, prophetic callings, angelic visitations, prophetic narratives, and indirect references to

the phenomena of dreams and visions comprise roughly one-third of the Bible.

In most accepted Bible concordances, there are 224 direct references to dreams and visions. I find that approximately 90 center on dreams in sleep while the remainder fall into the category of visions, which are merely dreams while you are awake. The belief that God speaks to us through dreams is both biblical and experiential.

Q: Where in the Bible should I look for a biblical perspective on dreams?

A: There are so many wonderful examples of dreams and dream interpretation in the Bible that it would take much too much space to cover them all here. However, let me give you a few, along with the gist of the dreams.

PILATE AND HIS WIFE

The Bible verse that first caught my attention and drew me to study the topic of God's relationship to dreams was Matthew 27:19. This is a very distinct New Testament passage concerning the persecution and ultimate death of Jesus. You may recall that Pilate was serving in his role as judge over Jesus when he received a message from his wife. The message read: "Don't have anything to do with that innocent man, for I have suffered a great deal today in a dream because of him."

The $64,000 question is, What was the origin of her dream? Since we know virtually nothing about her, or her relationship to God or with Jesus, we must assume only three possibilities exist. One, which I discount, is that she was lying. The second possibility is that her dream came directly from God. The last possibility is that she dreamed it on her own with no divine intervention.

My hypothesis is that given what we know of Pilate's position regarding Jesus, coupled with his preoccupation with the political instead of spiritual ramifications of putting Jesus to death, we can surmise that he was spiritually shut off from Jesus. Carrying out this reasoning, we could then postulate that he was not a candidate to receive a message from God concerning Jesus whether he was awake, asleep, or eating donuts while climbing trees.

Since we know next to nothing about Pilate's wife, we can only guess that she was *somewhat* like-minded. Let's stipulate, though, that by the very nature of the fact that she had a dream about Jesus and the wrong about to be imposed on Him, she must have possessed a higher sense of spirituality or at least a sense of right and wrong.

I would conclude that she wasn't troubled enough emotionally during her waking hours to generate a thought of the magnitude that would cause her to send a warning letter to her husband. Instead, it's more plausible to believe that God found spiritually deaf ears in Pilate and therefore chose his wife to impart a warning dream, knowing she possessed enough spirituality to at least deliver the message to Pilate. The rest, as they say, is history.

JOSEPH, THE FIRST DREAM ANALYST

A second tremendous scriptural study into dreams can be found in the story of Joseph (Gen. 37–50). Let me give you just a flavor of how rich these verses are in dreams and dream interpretation while I encourage you to read the entire passage for yourself.

Joseph relayed a most interesting dream to his dear eleven brothers: "Listen to this dream I had: We were binding sheaves of grain out in the field when suddenly my sheaf rose and stood upright, while your sheaves gathered around mine and bowed down to it" (Gen. 37:6–7).

Then Joseph had another dream, and guess what? Right, he told this one to his brothers as well: "Listen . . . I had another dream, and this time the sun and moon and eleven stars were bowing down to me" (Gen. 37:9).

When you get into the story, you'll learn that Joseph's brothers were less than pleased with their little brother and his dreams. In fact, they were so fed up with his dreams and the way that their parents (particularly their father) seemed to favor Joseph over them, they plotted against him and sold their little brother into slavery for twenty shekels—or about the cost of two Happy Meals today.

The important thing was that Joseph's prophetic dreams were his first introduction to God's plan in his life. He didn't know it at the time, but God was telling him that His big plans for Joseph would include ruling Egypt and eventually having his brothers bow down to him in acknowledgment of his greatness and authority. You will find that Joseph's first dream of the sheaves of grain all bowing down to him along with his second dream of the sun (father) and moon (mother) and eleven stars (brothers) bowing down came true.

What is even more interesting in the study of dreams is how Joseph used his gifts and abilities to analyze dreams as a means of getting close to Pharaoh and ultimately gaining Pharaoh's trust. Joseph's life is a marvelous study in dream symbols and the way that God speaks through dreams.

DANIEL BECOMES AN AUTHORITY ON DREAMS

As you look into the Bible's messages on dreams, you must examine Daniel and his gift of dream interpretation (Dan. 2–11). A particularly note-worthy aspect of Daniel's story is that he is described as sort of an ordinary guy. Let me explain. When King Nebuchadnezzar had his series of bewildering dreams, the Bible described his mind-set as "troubled" and he could not sleep. In an attempt to remedy this, Nebuchadnezzar summoned the usual cast of characters, including magicians, enchanters, sorcerers, and astrologers, to explain what he had dreamed. The problem was that the top four in his batting order all whiffed! They struck out and could not reveal what the king's dreams meant.

That was where our friend Daniel entered, and please take note that he was introduced not as a magician, enchanter, sorcerer, or astrologer, but as a *wise man* (not to be confused with one of the three wise men from the birth of Jesus stories). In the parlance of the time, that meant he was highly regarded and sought out as a wise counselor. Keep in mind that Daniel was not given to cheap parlor tricks, common with those listed above, and would not resort to guessing or trickery when interpreting Nebuchadnezzar's dreams. In fact, in Daniel 2:30, he described himself as having no greater wisdom than anybody else. In other words, Daniel said he was just a "regular" guy, but he was going to interpret the dreams so that the king could understand it.

Whether God spoke through Daniel directly to interpret the king's dreams, or Daniel possessed a spiritual gift of interpreting dreams, rest assured, he was a master dream analyst. Evidence would point to Daniel's using a spiritual gift since he played such a major role in prophecy and was such a prophetic dreamer.

GOD SPEAKS TO JOSEPH THROUGH DREAMS

Another marvelous New Testament study into dreams comes in the beloved and miraculous story of the virgin birth (Matt. 1:18–25). In it we see that Joseph (not the same Joseph we explored in Genesis) was struggling mightily over the moral issue of how to handle the fact that his betrothed, Mary, was with child. It wasn't until an angel of the Lord appeared in his dream that he knew what path he must take to provide for Mary and the unborn baby Jesus. Again, as with previous examples, Joseph was an "ordinary guy" who was placed in an "extraordinary" situation and then given direction from God through dreams.

To sum it up, certainly biblical research and Christian experience confirm that God does indeed use dreams to reveal Himself and to offer His loving guidance. For those who have taken the challenge to explore their own dreams with prayer and spiritual direction have found the goodness and faithfulness of the Lord in a new way.

Note to reader: the intent of this section is not to chronicle the multitude of biblical references to dreams and visions. The best way to research dreams is to use a concordance, topical index Bible, or word-search Bible computer program, and then read the accounts provided.

Q: How do I know if a dream is from God?

A: Any teachings that do not pass the test of biblical support and reference should be viewed with skepticism. Most likely you will never be 100 percent sure until you are one day afforded the luxury of asking God yourself. There are some guidelines I've developed over the years for *testing the spirit* of dreams:

PRAY

Pray about your dream. Ask God to confirm or deny that your dream is from Him. He may give you a similar dream, He may speak to you through specific Scriptures that may leap right off the page, or He may speak through others.

TEST YOUR SPIRIT

Consider carefully how you felt when you awakened from the dream. A common theme among those experiencing divine dreams is that they will immediately sense God's presence in some way. Another test of your spirit is to get the sense of whether your dream made you feel closer to or more distant from God. Dreams that draw you closer to God are more likely to be divinely inspired. Dreams that drive a wedge between you and your faith are not.

SEEK OUT A MULTITUDE OF COUNSELORS (PROV. 11:14)

Sometimes a multitude of counselors can flat out make you crazy. But in the spirit of Proverbs 11:14, seeking select counsel and advice from other Christians can be valuable if you know the spirit of the person or persons whose counsel you are seeking. For their counsel to be valuable in this area, they must at least be open to the fact that God may speak through dreams today, as He did in the Bible.

ASK, "DOES MY DREAM ALIGN WITH SCRIPTURE?"

I once received a call from a criminal defense attorney who asked me if I'd be willing to testify that it's at least *possible* that Jesus, through a dream, told his client to commit a murder. I respectfully declined, not because it wasn't a possibility that Jesus spoke to the man in his dream, but because it was *impossible* to accept that Jesus would contradict God's first commandment against committing murder.

EVALUATE THE DREAM CONTENT

Examine the content of the dream. Even though it may be hidden beneath multiple dream symbols and themes, does your dream glorify Jesus? If it does, this is another positive indication.

DETERMINE WHETHER THE DREAM IS CONSISTENT WITH OTHER SPIRITUAL LEADINGS

I met with a man who revealed a dream in which God appeared to him and directed him to travel to a foreign land to serve as a missionary. He wanted to know if it was, in fact, God who appeared in his dream. I asked him if, prior to the dream, he felt led to become a missionary. Or had he received counsel from his pastor, church elders, or others that this was something he should pursue? He answered a resounding *yes*. What that tells me is that there is a consistency between his dream, the desires of his heart, and the wisdom and counsel of his elders. That tends to erase the doubts concerning divine authorship of a dream.

Q: Does everyone dream?

A: Yes. Laboratory studies have shown that everyone dreams.

Q: Do you dream in color or in black and white?

A: Both, although most people dream in color. There seems to be a connection between vivid high-color dreaming and people who are imaginative, artistic, and creative.

Q: I've heard the term *REM sleep*. What is it?

A: Our most vivid dreams take place during a type of sleep called rapid eye movement (REM) sleep. During REM stages, the brain is very active, the eyes move back and forth rapidly under the lids, and the large muscles of the body are relaxed. REM sleep generally takes place every 90 to 100 minutes, 3 to 4 times a night, and lasts longer as the night progresses. The final REM period may last as long as 45 minutes. Less vivid dreams occur at other times during the night.

Q: Why do some people have trouble remembering their dreams?

A: Some people have no difficulty remembering several dreams nightly, while others can't recall dreams at all. Most of what happens during sleep—including dreams, the thoughts occurring throughout the night, and memories of brief awakenings—is forgotten by morning. There is something about the phenomenon of sleep that makes it difficult to remember what has occurred in dreams. Many people, upon awakening, report they did not dream, although sometime later in the day, or even another day, they remember a dream. This might suggest that the memory, during sleep, is not totally lost but for some reason is hard to retrieve.

Q: Can food, alcohol, or medicine affect dreams?

A: Sleep—and therefore dreams—is affected by a great variety of drugs and medications, including alcohol. Furthermore, stopping or starting certain medications may cause nightmares. There is no clinical evidence to support the old wives' tale that a large (or spicy) meal before bedtime brings about more dreams.

Q: Are there ways I can improve my dream memory?

A: Generally yes. As you are saying your prayers, ask God to help you remember any dreams that you may have, and tell Him that you are just as open to listening to Him through your dreams as you are while awake.

Then before you fall asleep, remind yourself that you want to remember your dreams. If you're serious about remembering and analyzing your dreams, keep a journal and a pen or tape recorder by your bedside. As you awaken, try to move as little as possible, and don't let your mind drift to your upcoming day. Write down all of your dreams and images because they can fade quickly if not recorded. Any distractions will cause the memory of your dream to fade. If you can't remember a full dream, record the last thing that was on your mind before awakening, even if you have only a vague memory of it.

Q: What does it mean to have a dream again and again?

A: This is a *recurrent dream*, and you saw many illustrations of this through the book. It's not unusual for recurrent dreams to continue for weeks, months, and even years. Understanding the meaning of a recurrent dream is generally more difficult because the fact that it has gone on for some time usually means one of two things. The more likely is that it stems from an earlier emotional scar that has not healed and still requires attention. The second is that it is a God-ordained dream, and He is revisiting it or the dreamer has not acted on it.

Q: Is it possible to die in your sleep if you die in your dream?

A: *Absolutely not!* This is an old wives' tale. I've spoken with hundreds of people who have had dreams where they die. As close as I can tell, they're alive and kicking while relaying their dreams to me. Falling, hitting bottom, crashing, and dying are all dream symbols and should be explored like any other dream symbol.

Q: Are the only meaningful dreams the ones from God?

A: Absolutely not! Although scientists don't seem to agree on what color the sky is, most agree that dreams are very meaningful. Most people who work with their dreams, either by themselves or with others, find that their dreams produce valuable insights. Aside from the opportunity to hear God's voice, dreams are useful in learning more about the dreamer's feelings, thoughts, behavior, motives, and values. There are numerous documented cases of people, especially artists, writers, or scientists, who often derive creative ideas from dreams. For instance, Jack Nicklaus credits a dream with fixing his golf swing, Lyndon Johnson decided not to run for president in 1968 because of a dream, and Harriet Tubman credited many of the routes for the Underground Railroad to her dreams.

Q: Is it difficult to interpret dreams?

A: At first it is perplexing, but not too difficult. In time, however, interpreting your dreams will become as comfortable as speaking with an old friend. The most important thing to keep in mind is that your dreams are images of your underlying thoughts, feelings, and anxieties—especially any anxieties—that you are not addressing while awake.

All of the people, actions, settings, and emotions in your dreams are personal to you. While some dream experts will tell you that there are typical or archetypal dreams and dream elements that remain constant to all people, others will maintain that images or symbols will have different meanings for different people. For example, a snake in a dream can mean one thing to a reptile lover and something quite different to a child. Furthermore, take that same snake symbol, which denotes sexual anxieties in Freudian analysis, and ask the evangelical Christian what a snake or serpent represents to him. You'll likely find that a serpent represents fear of being led astray, deceived, or distanced from God. This is precisely why I assert that secular dream symbol dictionaries have very little relevance in the lives of people of faith and why I have been working on one for several years.

The best way to start analyzing your dream is to think about what each dream element and symbol in your dream means to you or what it reminds you of in your life. By looking for connections between your dream associations and what is happening in your waking life, and by being patient and persistent, you can learn to understand your dreams.

Q: Are nightmares normal?

A: Yes, they are very common in early childhood, but start to dissipate thereafter. It's been my experience that about 50 percent of adults report having at least one disturbing nightmare within the last six months. Generally speaking, stress, traumatic events, emotional struggles, use of drugs or medication, or illness may trigger nightmares.

Q: Can dreams predict the future?

A: Predictive dreaming is a very difficult issue. On the one hand, I've worked with a multitude of patients and heard from dozens more about dreams that they claim have predicted the future. As a scientist, I'd pass much of this off to coincidence or faulty memory. On the other hand, if God were to speak through a dream about a future event, that event would happen unless He ordained differently. From a clinical perspective, a few laboratory studies have been conducted of predictive dreams as well as clairvoyant and telepathic dreams, but the results were inconclusive. I can assure you, however, that these scientists were not open to the possibility of God speaking through dreams.

Q: Is it possible to control dreams?

A: There is a technique called *preconditioning (or pre-sleep suggestions)* whereby studies have shown that dreamers can determine the types and/or outcomes of certain dreams. This, of course, would not apply to any dreams ordained by God. Another method of influencing dreams is called *lucid dreaming,* in which you are aware you are dreaming while still asleep and in the dream. It is often possible to learn how to increase lucid dreaming and thereby increase your capacity to affect the course of the dream events as they unfold. Generally I would suggest that it is not only difficult to control your dreams, but also inadvisable. Instead, doesn't it make more sense to encourage learning from the dream rather than trying to control it?

A FINAL ENCOURAGEMENT

I've cherished the opportunity to share not only some of the hundreds of dream stories I've collected over the years, but also something about myself, my faith, and my philosophy. Ultimately I pray you came away from this experience with two gifts pertaining to dreams.

The first gift is that you now have a heightened awareness of the role that dreams play in revealing your hidden thoughts, desires, feelings, emotions, and collective past. The second is an understanding of how God has used dreams throughout the Bible and that He could be speaking directly to you through your dreams.

I've heard Christians say that they wonder what's wrong with them because they don't hear God in their dreams or sense His leading. You should *never* second-guess your faith, your relationship with God, or your commitment to Him simply because you don't yet receive divine dreams. The truth is that some of you reading this book will undoubtedly encounter God in future dreams while others may not. This isn't a reflection on you or your spirituality. Dreams are just one method of communication at God's discretion. If you don't hear Him in your dreams now, then look and listen to Him in other areas of your life. At the same time, however, pray about God's presence in your dreams, and then keep alert to see what transpires.

We know from studying spiritual gifts (1 Cor. 12:4) that each believer has at least one special gift. No single gift is more precious than the others. Therefore, if you don't find God in your dreams, keep searching, but don't lose faith in the process. Instead, seek out your other spiritual gift(s) and use it (or them) for God.

At the same time that I encourage you to become more aware of your dreams, I want to provide a word of caution. Please do not allow yourself to be enticed into the New Age movement because followers of that movement talk about the importance of dreams. Any dialogue of dreams that isn't grounded in Scripture and followed with biblical principles should be viewed as secular-humanistic and worldly. In the study of dreams it's nearly impossible to avoid the secular-humanistic and worldly psychological perspective. Anytime you read or hear that you can become God, you are equal to God, or you can tune in to God whenever you choose through your dreams, run away. Without a doubt the easiest way to stay out of danger is to stay grounded in your faith by reading and studying your Bible. I encourage you to attend a mainstream Bible-teaching church, and seek the advice and counsel of pastors and mature Christians.

FOR MORE INFORMATION
ON YOUR DREAMS . . .

WEB SITE

You can reach Dr. Cynaumon via the Internet at www.dreamfocus.org. If you are interested in submitting your dream to Dr. Cynaumon, please go to www.dreamfocus.org and follow the online instructions. The Web site www.dreamfocus.org also features speaking engagement booking information, and an active dream-posting chat room where you may submit your dreams and converse with others who are interested in dream interpretation from both a psychological and a Christian perspective.

Dr. Cynaumon's additional dream books, tapes, and resources are also available at this Web site. If you'd like to be placed on Dr. Cynaumon's mailing list to receive free updates and newsletters, please go to www.dreamfocus.org and simply leave your name and address.

FUTURE BOOKS

Dr. Cynaumon is currently working on the sequel to this book as well as a dream symbol dictionary specifically tailored to Christians and a dream interpretation training book. Be sure to look for them at your local bookstore, or visit www.dreamfocus.org.

ABOUT THE AUTHOR

G REG CYNAUMON, Ph.D., a nationally recognized expert on families, marriage, and counseling issues, is perhaps best known as the co-creator of *The Phonics Game*, a home reading program. He has developed games and toys for Focus on the Family, Hasbro, Mattel, and for his own company, Family Games, Inc. His products include *The Dr. Laura Game;* and *Left Behind* the board game. Cynaumon has been a frequent guest on national television and radio programs including *Montel Williams, 700 Club,* and *PTL,* and has made appearances on CNBC and FOX Network News. His previous books include *Barnes and Noble's Bible Trivia Quiz Book, Helping Single Parents with Troubled Kids, Empowering Single Parents,* and *How to Avoid Alienating Your Kids in 10 Easy Steps.* He lives in Los Angeles with his wife, Jan, and their daughter and son.